rt ʼ DC

Practical Drama and Theatre Arts

Studymates

British History 1870–1918
Warfare 1792–1918
Hitler and Nazi Germany (3rd Edition)
English Reformation
European History 1870–1918
Genetics (2nd edition)
Lenin, Stalin and Communist Russia
Organic Chemistry (2nd Edition)
Chemistry: As Chemistry Explained
Chemistry: Chemistry Calculations Explained
The New Science Teacher's Handbook
Mathematics for Adults
Calculus
Understanding Forces
Algebra: Basic Algebra Explained
Plant Physiology
Poems to Live By
Shakespeare
Poetry
Better English
Better French
Better German
Better Spanish
Social Anthropology
Statistics for Social Science
Practical Drama
The War Poets 1914–18
The Academic Essay
Your Master's Thesis
Your PhD Thesis

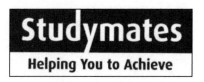

Studymates
Helping You to Achieve

Practical Drama and Theatre Arts

David Chadderton

www.studymates.co.uk

© 2006 by David Chadderton
© 2006 additional website reviews Studymates Limited.

ISBN 10 1-84 285-082-2
ISBN 13 978 1-84 285-082-4

First published in 2006 by Studymates Limited.
PO Box 225, Abergele, LL18 9AY, United Kingdom.

Website: http://www.studymates.co.uk

Typeset by Domex e-Data Pvt. Ltd.
Printed and bound in Great Britain by Baskerville Press

Contents

Introduction

The aim of this book is to teach about theatre through practical activities. In most cases, these activities are grouped into areas associated with the creation and production of theatre. While a number of books list games and exercises or schemes of work based around certain themes or issues – which are all useful for drama teachers and group leaders – the approach used here is to teach practical skills that can later be applied to any project with which the reader becomes involved. The skills taught will be useful for anyone learning theatre skills at 'Exam Level' or for private drama examinations as well as for anyone involved with drama groups, drama clubs and amateur theatre companies.

I would like to thank a few people for helping to make this book possible. Firstly a big thank you to Paul Heap, Head of Drama at Tormead School in Guildford, for reading and commenting on the manuscript as it was being written, for his encouragement and for being a good friend for a number of years. Thank you to Barry Carr, Company Director of Mainstream Theatre Arts, for his encouragement and occasional advice and for allowing me time to write this book. Thanks also to Paul Metcalf for originally getting me interested in and involved with live sound. Thanks are also due to a number of tutors and former tutors of Rose Bruford College who opened my mind so much to what theatre can be, including Chris Baldwin, Chris Megson, Michael Walling, Tony Coult, Susan Melrose, Elaine Turner and Jean Benedetti, and especially to Professor Anthony Hozier, Vice Principal, who still finds time to encourage me in everything I do despite being so busy with his remarkable work at the college. I am also very grateful to Denise Piguet of Rosco and Celia Jones of Shure for providing some of the images for this edition. And of course a big thank you to Lindsey Wright for encouraging me, for putting up with me, and for still being there when I emerge blinking from behind the computer screen.

David Chadderton
Email: *david.chadderton@Studymates.co.uk*

**Liverpool
Community
College**

What is Theatre?

Attempting to define theatre

The empty space

Theatre is about action, so we will immediately begin with an exercise.

Brainstorm – what is theatre?

A 'brainstorm' is a great method of finding initial ideas on a subject and can be done alone or in a group. For this technique to work, every idea that occurs to you about the subject must be written down without judgment; only after the brainstorm can you examine the ideas and discard the ones you do not like. For this exercise we will use the title of this chapter, so write 'What is theatre?' in the middle of a large sheet of paper. Now write around this title anything shouted out by members of the group that they associate with theatre. When you have as many words and phrases as you can think of or that will fit on the paper, you can look through your suggestions and pick out the ones that you think are important in defining what theatre means to you.

This is not an exercise with a fixed answer, as it will reflect your own experiences of theatre. As you proceed through this book, look back occasionally to your list and see whether your ideas have changed.

Theatre can be many things, and to define it can limit its scope. To some it is the red velvet curtains and ornate architecture of Victorian and Edwardian theatres, large-scale musicals, Shakespeare or a place to relax and be entertained. To others, theatre is a forum for political and social debate where real social change can be instigated. Some confusion arises from the fact that the word 'theatre' refers both to a building and to the activity that goes on inside it, but they are separable and do not depend on one another. Theatre does not need theatres; it can exist on the street or in a studio, park, school hall, field, old barn or abandoned warehouse – any setting where a group of actors and spectators come together for the purpose of creating theatre. Director Peter Brook boils theatre down to its two essentials of actor and spectator in the opening of his seminal 1968 book *The Empty Space*: 'I can take any empty space and call it a bare stage. A man walks across this empty space whilst someone else is watching him, and this is all that is needed for an act of theatre to be engaged'.

Theatre v. TV and cinema

Why do we need theatre any more? Surely there's nothing that can be done in the theatre that can't be done better in film or on television?

Whenever technology produces a new art form, the death knell is rung for the older art form that it is supposed to have replaced. Photography was said to be the death of painting; cinema was to wipe out live theatre; television would replace cinema. Although in each case there were significant effects on the older art form, all survived and were transformed by the experience. For instance, painting was no longer needed to document real life and to accurately recreate reality, so it took a completely different direction. It could portray moods, feelings, atmosphere and symbols or even be purely decorative without any need to be 'realistic'.

Theatre is still undergoing this transition, and a great deal of it still tries to mimic cinema in attempting to give an accurate portrayal of real life. However, this greatly limits what theatre can show and many of the elements unique to theatre are seen as limitations. Some practitioners see these features as assets that can allow theatre to penetrate real life more deeply than would be possible by just showing a 'slice of life' on the stage. Naturalism, the artistic movement that tried to create accurate copies of real life, was an important movement in theatre in the late 19th and early 20th centuries and is still a huge influence. It is important to realise, however, that realism is just one of many possible styles; saying that a piece of drama is 'not realistic' does not necessarily mean that there is something wrong with it. Non-naturalistic styles can, in many circumstances, be at least as effective as naturalism and often more so.

Cinema and television are created once and then may be shown repeatedly, but theatre is recreated anew at each performance for each audience and will be slightly different from any other performance. When you watch a performance in the theatre, you can be sure that what you see is being created live for you and will never have been seen before and will never be seen again in quite the same way. Theatre is also a two-way medium; the performance is affected just as much by the reactions of the audience as it is by the actions of the performers. When Hamlet turns to the audience on stage and asks, 'To be, or not to be?' he is asking that audience at that moment to consider the question of whether he should live or die. When we see Olivier or Branagh or Mel Gibson ask this question on film, we know that they were looking at a camera and creating a performance for anyone who might see it, not just for you at the moment you are watching. This is where theatre can be so much more powerful than any recorded medium, even if it does not always achieve this power.

Theatre and cinema

Look at the following headings and consider what are the advantages and limitations of theatre and cinema for each of them. Think carefully about each one beyond the obvious – for instance, it may be obvious that cinema can create better special effects, but seeing a clever magic trick live before your eyes can be so much more impressive than seeing it on film when camera trickery could easily be involved.

1. Special visual effects.
2. Documentary-style look at family life.
3. Examining what a character thinks but does not say.
4. Making the spectators feel as though they are actually there.
5. A story that moves between many different locations.

Theatre from the past

Theatre history

Examining the theatres of the past can help us to understand how our own theatre works and even how to make it work better. It is also very important, if we are to produce a play from a past era, that we know where it came from and how its first audiences would have received it, as this is an important part of the play's meaning (although this does not mean that the original conditions have to be copied to put over the same meaning to a modern audience).

A block for modern audiences and readers of plays from the past is that they are often taught and produced as something sombre, serious and difficult to watch. Ancient Greek plays are often translated by poets or Greek scholars rather than theatre practitioners; Shakespeare is often taught in schools on the page as poetic writing rather than as living theatre. These plays were written to be performed live on a stage in eras when theatre was central to society, filled with colour, music, dancing and song, attended by all from slaves to high priests, from young apprentices to lords. While it is useful and interesting to look at Shakespeare's use of rhyme, verse, alliteration and so on, his real genius was in using these literary devices to create characters and stories that came to life on a stage for his audiences and are still telling us things about ourselves 400 years later.

Ancient Greek theatre spaces

Greek society

The fifth century BCE was the golden era of Greek theatre, producing the great tragedy writers Aeschylus, Sophocles and Euripides and the comedy writer Aristophanes. After thousands of years of living in small tribes, within a few generations the city of Athens had grown up with a population of around 6,000 people. This sudden collision of many people together produced a crisis of identity, but also one of the most creative periods of human history. This is when the foundations of modern theatre, democratic government, science, mathematics, astronomy, literature and philosophy were created – and these still form the foundation of western civilisation and learning. It was also a very violent time and many people were killed by wars and plagues. The place in which many issues were debated and where religion and society were examined was the theatre.

The appearance of theatre

The origins of theatre are thought to be in annual rural fertility festivals. According to legend, theatre was born from choral singing and storytelling, when one person stepped from the chorus to act out the story and debate issues with the rest of the chorus. This first actor was said to be called Thespis, and actors are sometimes still referred to as 'thespians'. It is thought that Aeschylus introduced a second actor into his plays, and Sophocles a third.

The great plays of Greek drama were performed at a festival in honour of the god Dionysus in which playwrights competed for a prize for the best play. Each writer selected for the festival had to write three tragedies and a 'satyr' – a low comedy that often ridiculed the same themes, characters or gods portrayed in the tragedies. To refer to these people simply as 'playwrights' diminishes their actual role in creating the drama. As well as writing four plays, they would also do the jobs of (in the modern theatre) the director, composer, choreographer and lead actor. Aeschylus lived to be around 69 years old and wrote at least 80 plays, only six of which survive (*Prometheus Bound* is also often ascribed to Aeschylus but its authorship is disputed).

Greek theatre was central to Greek society in a way that we cannot imagine today. First of all it was primarily a religious festival that everyone would have been expected to attend. The audience consisted of the whole of society: men and women; slaves and masters; everyone from the poorest workers to the richest merchants. The chorus (a group of performers responsible for telling the story to the audience) was made up of amateur performers taken from the citizens of Athens and the productions were financed by a rich citizen in return for a tax-free year (which would not have reimbursed his costs).

Greek plays were usually based on Greek mythology, often from the poems of the great Greek poet Homer, although the plays often changed or disputed the established myths in order to make audiences question their beliefs and society. Greek comedy poked fun at Greek myths and society and would even mercilessly mock important people who were sat in the audience. This causes a problem for us now when looking at the plays because Greek mythology and society is not something most modern audiences will know a great deal about. Its original audience would have been at least as familiar with it as a modern Western audience is with the Christmas and Easter stories. Greek theatre was filled with music, song and dance and bright colours, but unfortunately it is rarely produced like this today.

Developing Greek theatre

- One person stands up and tells a story. This can either be a well-known story – fairy tales can be useful for this – or something that has happened to that person. This where theatre came from: people standing before an audience telling stories.

- The same person repeats the story, but this time one other person plays all of the people in the story and speaks their words (including the person telling the story if it is about them). Think about how the actor can play each character in a different way to distinguish between them. The Greeks used different masks to help with this.
- The story is repeated a third time, but this time with two actors playing different roles.

Each of these three methods tells exactly the same story; the difference is how the story is presented. How does each method give the audience a different experience of the story?

These three very simple steps actually represent giant leaps in the development of theatre performance.

- Step one is simple storytelling, which is at the heart of every theatre performance and is still a popular form, from bedtime stories for young children and books for children and adults read out on the radio to the growing popularity of the audiobook. Storytelling is a performance in which one person or group communicates a story to another person or group using the spoken word.
- Step two represents the creation of theatre. Instead of the storyteller describing everything that happens in words, some actions can be demonstrated to the audience by the actor instead. Storytelling has gained a visual component instead of being exclusively verbal. The storytellers still have an important role to play to tie everything together; in Greek theatre they were known as the chorus.
- Step three represents the creation of modern drama (including theatre, cinema and television). With two actors, whole scenes can be created in which characters interact with one another without any need for explanation from the chorus. The story is suddenly put into the present tense; instead of being told about something that has happened, the spectators see it happening now in front of them. The chorus may still be

used – as a chorus, a narrator, a voice-over or as screen titles, for example – but it has become an optional tool rather than the main method of communicating the story.

Greek theatres

The Greek theatre was in the open air and consisted of three main components:

1. **Orchestra** – literally 'dancing space'. This was a circular space in which the main action of the play took place. There was an altar somewhere in the orchestra to the god Dionysus.
2. **Theatron** – literally 'seeing place'. This was the seating area that surrounded approximately three quarters of the orchestra and rose upwards. Originally wooden, the later theatres had stone seating.
3. **Skene** – literally 'tent', which is probably what it originally was. This was a low building at the back of the orchestra in which the actors changed. It was used to represent different types of buildings in the plays and actors would enter and exit through it, use it as a backdrop to their acting or even appear on its roof. A wheeled platform called the *ekkuklema* could be brought out of the skene with a scene already set on it, often with dead bodies on it (many Greek plays contain some quite horrific violence, but it would always happen offstage).

**Fig. 1:
Greek theatre
layout**

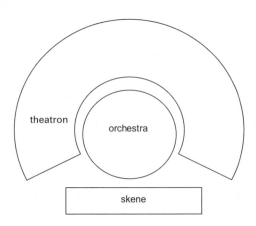

Theatre in Renaissance London

Renaissance London

The word 'renaissance' means a revival, and the Renaissance was a revival of Greek and Roman art, culture and thinking that swept Europe from as far back as the 12th century up to the early 17th century. Mediaeval European theatre, like Classical Greek theatre, had been tied very closely to religion, re-enacting stories from the Bible in churches or public spaces. During the Renaissance, the theatre cut its ties to the church and began to tell all kinds of stories.

Renaissance London, like Classical Athens, was a place of great change. Between 1550 and 1650 the population of London grew from 120,000 to 375,000 people. This was an age of great discoveries in global exploration, science and the arts. Merchants from all over the world were coming to London to buy and sell goods. It was also a time when the plague was killing many thousands of people, and there was great political and religious turmoil that eventually resulted in the English Civil War. In the midst of all this were the London theatres, attended by all sections of society from the young apprentices to the aristocracy.

Public theatres

The public theatres in London were based on a circular shape like the Greek theatres, although they were modelled more on the inn courtyards where groups of travelling players (as actors were called at this time) would perform. The orchestra of the Greek theatre became the pit, where the majority of the audience stood around the raised stage to watch the performance. The stage extended out from the tiring house, the equivalent of the skene, which had doors in the front of it for the actors to make their entrances. A highly-decorated canopy extended over the stage, which was known as the heavens. The theatron was replaced by balconies that sat on top of one another, containing seats for the wealthier patrons. There are a number of reconstructions of Elizabethan theatres around the world of varying authenticity, the best being Shakespeare's Globe in London, which is well worth a visit.

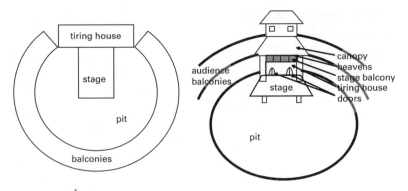

Fig. 2:
Basic diagrams
of an Elizabethan
playhouse

Although some quite elaborate and expensive costumes were worn, not much scenery was used – you may have noticed if you have studied any of Shakespeare's plays that characters often describe where they are, how light it is and even what the weather is like for the audience's benefit. Performances were in daylight, which creates a completely different level of actor-audience communication than if audiences are plunged into darkness. Although the chorus was rarely used – Shakespeare sometimes used a character he called 'Chorus' to introduce a play – there were moments within the plays when the actors spoke directly to the audience. Two common devices for this are:

1. **The soliloquy** – a character alone on stage speaks his or her thoughts directly to the audience, often coming to a major decision.
2. **The aside** – a comment directly to the audience during a scene revealing what a character is really thinking, which the other characters in the scene do not hear.

Asides

In pairs, start up a conversation as though you are two people who have just met after not seeing each other for a long time. On the surface you are both polite, but you don't really like each other. Every time you say something to the other person, turn to the audience and tell them what you really think!

Modern theatre spaces

Types of space

The following are the most common types of theatre space in use today.

1. **End stage** – this is simply a stage at one end of a room with the audience sat facing it. A common type of end stage is the proscenium stage, which has a proscenium arch (from the Greek *proskene* or 'in front of the *skene*') or picture frame surrounding the stage through which the audience views the action. There may be an area of stage extending in front of the proscenium arch called an apron.
2. **Theatre-in-the-round, or arena stage** – as the name suggests, this is a circular acting space with the audience seated all around.
3. **Thrust** – the audience is seated on three sides of the acting space. The thrust can be the whole stage or an acting area extending from the main stage like a catwalk.
4. **Promenade** – different scenes are performed in different parts of the room, or even in different rooms or outside, and the audience walks from one scene to the next.
5. **Traverse** – the audience is seated on two opposing sides of the acting space.
6. **Found space** – this is theatre in a place that was not created for theatre performance, such as a barn, old factory or abandoned warehouse, which uses the original features of the building rather than converting it into a conventional theatre space.

Using space

Take any scene that you know – you could use the one you created for the exercise on Greek theatre or any scene from a play you have read or studied – and try to stage it for as many different types of acting space as you can. What are the special considerations you have to bear in mind for each type of space? For instance, when staging a play for theatre-in-the-round, each actor will

---

always have his or her back to a third of the audience and any scenery over a certain height will prevent some of the audience from seeing anything.

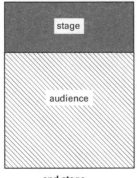

end stage

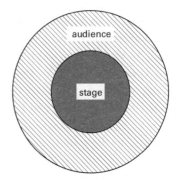

theatre-in-the-round

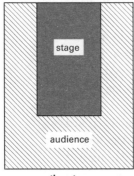

thrust

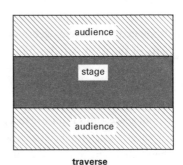

traverse

▲
**Fig. 3:
Modern stage
configurations**

Tutorial

Practice questions

1 For any play you have studied, explain how you would stage it:

a. for a proscenium stage

b. in-the-round

c. as promenade theatre.

Explain the special problems and considerations applicable to each.

2 What are the main problems with staging a play from a different period of history and what should a director do to overcome these problems?

3 Try to find information about the following types of historical theatres:

a. Mediaeval mystery plays

b. Restoration comedy

c. Commedia dell'arte.

Create your own exercises for investigating how to stage each of these theatre types.

Seminar discussion

How can a study of theatre history help us to understand and create modern theatre?

Study, revision and exam tips

1 Whenever you read a play script, try to work out how it could be staged in different ways and make notes.

2 Try to see theatre in as many different types of acting space as possible and make notes on how the play is staged to accommodate the space and how the different types of space affect the play and the audience differently.

2 Improvisation

One-minute overview

Improvisation is one of the fundamental tools of drama. It is often used in drama classes and rehearsals and can also be used to create whole performances either as they are performed or in rehearsals. Practical exercises in spontaneous and prepared improvisation, accepting and blocking and character status give performers the skills and confidence to be creative without having a script to lean on and extra tools to investigate script and character.

This chapter will cover:
- beginning improvisation
- improvisation techniques and exercises
- performing improvisation.

Beginning improvisation

The dictionary defines *improvisation* as 'something done or produced on the spur of the moment'. Improvisation in drama is created without the aid of a prepared script and sometimes without any preparation at all. In Britain, improvisation is often referred to as 'impro', whereas in America it is known as 'improv', particularly when referring to improvised comedy.

Improvisation is commonly used in classes to experiment with performance skills and techniques and in rehearsals to explore plot, setting and characterisation. It is also a performance skill in its own right; some productions are partly or wholly improvised or were created using improvisation during rehearsals.

Improvisation is about listening, not just about talking. When working from a script, it is easy to get into the habit of listening only for the familiar cue that tells you when it is your turn to speak. When improvising, actors have to listen carefully to each other, just as they would in a real-life situation, to know where the scene is taking them. Improvisers must work closely as a team and be prepared to go with whatever happens, even if they would have liked the scene to happen differently.

It is essential to create a good working atmosphere in the classroom, studio or rehearsal room. A group in which everyone competes to create the funniest lines or to play the best characters will not work well in improvisation (or in any form of drama). A group that works together to help each other through scenes and in which each member is prepared to take whichever role fits the scene being played has the potential to create some good work. If each person is totally committed to the group, work can be created by the group that no individual member could have created alone.

Initial doubts about improvisation

Why do we need to learn improvisation in drama? I've never seen a performance in the theatre that was improvised.

Improvised theatre does exist. Improvised comedy is very popular in comedy clubs in Britain and America, and has even got onto television with programmes like *Whose Line Is It Anyway?* on Channel 4 in the UK. Serious theatre created from improvisation also exists.

But surely this sort of thing happens only on the fringes of drama or in comedy. What use is it if I want to be a serious actor in straight drama?

Improvisation is also a very useful technique for rehearsing a text-based piece of theatre. Games and exercises are often used in rehearsal to help the actors (and the director) to get to the heart of a script. This may include creating scenes using the characters in situations other than those shown in the play, or creating a modern scene to parallel a scene in a historical piece to help the actors understand the scene. It is also a very useful tool for learning and practising various acting techniques.

I really just want to be a writer. Don't writers just sit in front of a typewriter or computer screen all day?

Many do, but improvisation is still often used in the creation of original drama. Much of the work done by directors such as Robert Lepage or by companies such as Theatre de Complicite began life as improvisation exercises. Max Stafford-Clark's company Joint Stock evolved a technique in which the writer and director would work with the cast using improvisation and discussion to put together ideas before the writer went away to write a script. The Writers' Group at the Royal Court Theatre in London in the 1950s used improvisation exercises with writers to help stimulate their imaginations and work through ideas. A scriptwriter must always be aware that he or she is creating a living piece of theatre, not just words on a page, and improvisation can help with this.

Ways into improvisation

The following exercises will get any group improvising quickly by creating stories on the spur of the moment as a group. You must remember to say the first thing that comes into your head when it is your turn without hesitating or trying to think of something 'good'. Those who try to be clever may get a laugh but they may also make it difficult for the story to continue.

The stories may not appear to make much sense, but they are *your* stories that *you* have made up without waiting for inspiration. Anyone who believes that they have no imagination may prove themselves wrong when they do these exercises. Do not try to tie the group down to situations that are realistic or sensible; if you allow your imagination to have free reign, your stories can travel through time and space, through the bodies of monsters, through death and back again.

For these exercises, get the whole group into a circle and take the story around the circle in order. If some members of the group are a bit wary of working in front of everyone else, start by working in pairs, all at the same time. As with any other skill, the more you practise these exercises with the same group, the more confident you will be with one another and the more you will develop your imagination.

Instant stories

One person gives the first line of a story. It can be as unusual ('Sir Olav packed his favourite dragon-killing lance and set off for the magical kingdom of Gulak') or as commonplace ('David climbed out of bed and went down for his breakfast') as you like, but do not try to lead how the story is supposed to go. The next person then has to come up with the next line of the story without hesitating. The story passes around the whole circle, several times if necessary, until it appears to come to a natural end. It can be more interesting if each person stops in the middle of a sentence that the next person has to complete, for instance, 'Bursting into the kitchen, he saw, sitting in the kitchen sink...'

When the group becomes more confident with this exercise, try it with each person pointing to the one who must follow them or with the group leader calling out the name or number of the next person instead of going round the circle. This means that everyone must remain alert and keep listening all the time instead of just when their turn is coming up.

Fortunately... unfortunately...

This is a variation of the 'Instant stories' exercise. The first person starts the story with the word 'Fortunately...' and something fortunate that happened. The next person starts with 'Unfortunately...' and then adds something unfortunate that progresses the story. As the story goes around the circle, you alternately get fortunate and unfortunate statements. You must remember that you are telling a story following on from the previous person, not just giving a list of fortunate and unfortunate events. For example, 'Fortunately, Joanne was going to pick up her new car,' 'Unfortunately, she clipped a parked car on the way home,' 'Fortunately, no one seemed to have noticed so she drove off,' 'Unfortunately, someone looking out of a window took her licence number,' etc.

One-word stories

This exercise sounds as though it could not possibly work, but it is surprising just how good the results can be. It can be very satisfying when a story created by a group in this way comes together.

One person starts the story by saying just one word. Again, do not try to say anything clever or imaginative. The next person says another single word that can follow the first. In this exercise, each person **must** say the first word that they think of; any hesitation can kill the momentum of the story. For instance, the first person may start with the word 'One...' The story may continue 'Day... John... Went... To... The... Bank... With... A... Gun...' Do not be frightened of starting new sentences – this exercise can often create huge sentences joined by numerous ands and buts.

Improvisation techniques and exercises

Accepting and blocking

The most common reason for an improvisation coming to a halt is that one of the actors has *blocked*. In other words, instead of *accepting* another person's idea and developing from it, this actor rejects the idea totally and does not offer a way of continuing the scene. For instance, in the story circle exercise above, a common block is when someone says, 'He died'. It is possible to develop from this, but it does not make it easy for the next person! The same sort of thing can happen in an improvised scene, for instance:

1st ACTOR: Excuse me, could you tell me where the post office is? [*Offer*]

2ⁿᵈ ACTOR: Sorry, I don't live around here. [*Block!*]

Or:

1ˢᵗ ACTOR: Your brother told me to wait for him here. [*Offer*]

2ⁿᵈ ACTOR: I don't have a brother. [*Block!*]

Unblocking

How could these scenes have been continued differently without blocking? As the scenes stand at the moment, what could the second actor in each case have added to their line to turn their block into a counter-offer?

People block for a variety of reasons, and in many cases they do not realise they are doing it until someone else points it out to them. They may not want the scene to go in the direction it seems to be going; they may be trying to give themselves the strongest part or the wittiest lines; they may unconsciously be unwilling to build on the other person's creativity; they may be being pushed towards playing a status (see below) that they are not comfortable with; the scene may be dealing with a subject they would prefer to avoid. Whatever the reason, the actor is failing to surrender to the needs of the dramatic situation and the scene grinds to a halt.

Look at this scene:

1ˢᵗ ACTOR: You'd better sit down.
[*Offer that sets mood for scene*]

2ⁿᵈ ACTOR: You know, don't you?
[*Accepts – the first line suggested that something is wrong*]

1ˢᵗ ACTOR: Know? How could I not know with all the scratches on the driver's door?
[*Accepts – picks up on the idea that 2ⁿᵈ actor has done something wrong and offers the idea that the car has been damaged*]

2ⁿᵈ ACTOR: That's one of the hazards of using a car for a bank robbery you see.
[*Accepts – takes the car idea and builds on it*]

In this case, neither actor knows what the other is going to come up with, but each builds on the creativity of the other. Each accepts a new idea introduced in the previous line and takes it further.

The best improvisers appear to be able to read each other's minds, but all they are doing is listening and accepting.

Completing the scene

How could this scene continue? Take the above dialogue and see how many ways you can think of to continue the scene.

Simple accepting exercise

This is a very simple exercise to be done in pairs or very small groups, all working at the same time. Each member of the group takes it in turns to start a scene with any line they choose. Their partner(s) must accept this line, however ridiculous it may seem, and continue the scene without pausing for thought. Let each scene play for around 30 seconds, then start a new scene with a different line.

As a development, instead of starting with a line, start with a movement or action, for example digging, putting on make-up, waking up and yawning, chopping something with an axe or peeping carefully into a box. The scene can continue using actions, dialogue or a combination of the two.

Over accepting

This exercise, which should be performed in pairs, can be enormously entertaining to watch. The first person says an apparently dull line to start the scene. The second person not only accepts this line, but also gives it far more importance than it appears to have. For instance, 'Have you been here long?' 'Long? You dare to ask me whether I've been waiting here long? I always have to wait for you. Ten years I've known you, and you have never been on time for anything. You know how much I wanted to see this film, and now I've missed the beginning. There's no point in going in now. I'll have to wait to see it on television.' The first person can now pick out something from this to over accept: 'You had to mention television, didn't you. You know how my mother loved that television. But I had no choice – I needed the money. She cast me out and refused to speak to me ever again. And now I have to live on the streets. You couldn't spare some change for a cup of tea could you?' 'Tea? 25 years I worked for that tea company...' And so on!

Hitchhiker with an attitude

This is a performance exercise for groups of around four people at a time. Set out four chairs to represent a car, and pick one person to play the driver. The driver stops and picks up the others (who play hitchhikers) one by one, a minute or so apart. Each hitchhiker must decide on an 'attitude' for their character, for example, sad, angry, frightened, happy or sinister. When each person enters the car, everyone else in the car must take on the attitude of the newcomer. For instance if the first hitchhiker is angry, the driver will also become angry when he or she is picked up. If the second is sad, the driver and the first hitchhiker also become sad. As you practise this exercise, try to give your character a reason for changing attitude (the second hitchhiker's reason for being sad may be totally different from the driver's and the first hitchhiker's reasons).

All improvisation exercises involve accepting. Create any scenario and give it to a group of actors to improvise, or just stand two people on stage and have one of them start any scene they wish. They will have to accept everything that the other performer does in order for the scene to succeed.

The following exercise is always popular, but you must make sure that each actor gets the chance to play each role so that everyone has the chance to get his or her own back on everyone else!

Two describe a third

This is a spontaneous improvisation exercise involving three people performing in front of the rest of the group.

Actors 1 and 2 are waiting for actor 3 to arrive. Actor 1 describes 3 to 2, talking about how 3 comes into the scene or situation they are playing as well as a physical description, unusual mannerisms, personality traits and so on. Note that you are not describing the real actor 3; you are setting up a character for them to play when they enter. When 3 comes in, he or she must play the character that has been described, to every detail. Actor 2 takes the responsibility for drawing out these traits (for example, if it has been said that 3 snorts like a pig when she laughs, 2 may tell her a joke).

Status

One of the most basic ways in which humans – or any social animals – relate to one another is through status. Watch a group of dogs, lions or baboons for a while and you will see patterns of aggression and submission that define the hierarchy of the group. In this way, the animals in the group create a structure that helps them to work together for survival.

Human beings use similar status exchanges to other animals, even if we are not always aware that this is what we are doing. This pattern of aggression and submission is obvious in violent situations, but it is present each time we interact with another person, and with animals too. When we pass another person on the street, patterns of looks and movements between us help us to decide how to pass in order that we don't walk straight into each other. When we fail to judge status correctly or both try to play the same status, it results in the 'pavement dance' where both keep stepping in the same direction. We insult our friends jokingly in conversation, raising our own status by reducing theirs, then we laugh to reduce ourselves again and to show that our act was not an aggressive one. In the same way, a dog may bark or growl and wag its tail at the same time when playing, allowing it to practise status-manipulation techniques while showing that it is not a threat.

All of us have a preferred status that we play in real life, although it can change depending on the situation we are in and to whom we are speaking. As an actor, it is very important to recognise what status you normally play and how you achieve this in order that you can modify your behaviour on stage. We have all built up an armoury of status devices to enable us to survive in social situations, and when we start to abandon them we can feel very vulnerable. However, this is essential for actors or they can only ever play slight variations of themselves. This is why it is so important to have a supportive atmosphere in a cast or class. Anyone who jokes about others' work can stop them from exploring these vulnerable areas, but the joker is also using a high-status trick to hide their own discomfort.

Investigating status in a group

Get the whole group to walk around the room at random, saying 'hello' to each person they pass.

What happens? The interaction looks and feels false, and the actors often laugh or try out different silly voices. They do not have a situation, so they aren't aware of what status they are supposed to be playing. In a real situation, they would be (perhaps unconsciously) aware of their status and would react naturally.

Now divide the group into two. This time, while walking around, one half of the group gets eye contact with each person they pass and holds it for three seconds. The other half gets eye contact, immediately looks away and then glances back. After a couple of minutes, swap over to give everyone a chance to experience both types of contact. It can be useful if at least one person just watches the exercise to observe the interaction and behaviour of the actors and how it changes.

What did the performers feel during this exercise? Did they feel differently when they were holding eye contact to when they were breaking it and looking back? Did the observer(s) notice any general differences in behaviour in each actor in the two parts of the exercise? This type of exercise is most effective if you find the answers to these questions by doing the practical exercise rather than by reading about it, so try it out before reading further.

Holding eye contact with someone is a high-status, aggressive act. Those who hold eye contact during this exercise often report feeling more powerful and observers see them striding around slowly and confidently. Breaking eye contact can also be high status if you are deliberately ignoring someone, but the look back implies nervousness and uncertainty. Those carrying out this action claim to feel vulnerable and nervous, which observers often see reflected in their quick movements and uncertain walk.

The tiniest of details can make a huge difference to the status you play. Try beginning each of your sentences with a very short 'er...' and see if others can spot what you are doing and how it alters your appearance. This hesitation is a low-status device that makes you appear hesitant and unsure of yourself and is an invitation for someone to interrupt you. Those who naturally play high-status often lengthen the 'er...' or turn it into an 'um...' and may not realise they are doing it until it is pointed out to them. A long 'er...' at the start of a sentence is a high-status device that indicates to others that you have something to say and you should not be interrupted.

Status gestures

Below is a list of other mannerisms. Copy this list and enter in the space opposite whether the mannerism is high or low status. Rather than just guessing, improvise conversations or scenes in pairs or small groups with one person trying out the mannerism. Although we can theorise about the effects, acting is about action and the power of these devices can only be seen by doing them. You will probably find that by doing one of these gestures, you naturally start to do others that imply a similar status, so make a note of these also if they are not on the list.

Touching face while speaking	
Keeping head very still while speaking	
Not looking at the person talking to you	
Speaking in complete sentences	
Speaking in short, incomplete sentences	
Sounding breathless while speaking	
Sitting back with legs apart	
Standing with toes pointing inwards	
Leaning forward while speaking	
Hunching shoulders forward	
Standing with a straight back, chest out	
Laughing while talking	
Constantly interrupting others	
Turning your back on the other person	

Were you surprised at any of your conclusions when you tried the gestures out in a scene? Did you have disagreements over any of them? Each one has an obvious answer, but they could all indicate the opposite status if they are performed differently. For instance, you may not be looking at the person talking to you because you are too frightened to look them in the eye or because you do not think their words are worth listening to.

Reversing status

Go through the same gestures and try to play each of them in a way that demonstrates the opposite status to the one you wrote down for the above exercise.

There are many different exercises you can use to practise status; in fact any scene you play, whether scripted or improvised, can be used to experiment with different status relationships. The following exercises ask you to play a similar scene using different status relationships and to examine the differences.

Status exercises from text

The following is a simple script that can be learned easily in order to perform the exercise. Do not try to do the exercise while holding scripts.

A: Well
B: Sorry
A: Sorry
B: That's it

This is a very simple scene between two people that does not tell us anything about the setting or characters. There is no punctuation, so any of the lines could be said as a question, an exclamation or a simple statement depending on the context.

Pairs of actors should learn and perform the script using all four status relationships:

A high and B low
B high and A low
A and B both high
A and B both low.

Observers should watch and point out to the actors anything they do that goes against the status they should be playing. Perform the scene again after the discussion and see if it can be improved upon.

Status exercises from improvisation

As with the above exercise, take a situation in pairs and improvise it using the four different status relationships. Try any of the following situations, or create your own:

- Two friends: one borrowed an item of clothing from the other and has damaged it.
- Boss and employee: the boss has to fire the employee.

- You suspect a parent/son/daughter/flatmate of reading your mail.
- A blind date.

When actors participate in these types of exercises, the status they play is often very high or very low. In real life, status differences usually tend to be much closer together and are constantly changing. The following exercises are designed to introduce more subtlety into status relationships.

Degrees of status

Prepare a pack of normal playing cards by taking out all of the face cards (jacks, queens and kings) and any jokers to leave a pack consisting of 40 number cards from one (ace) to ten. The cards are shuffled and each person in the group takes a card at random, unseen. The card indicates their status, from one (a cowering little mouse) to ten (the most powerful king in the universe). In pairs or small groups, improvise scenes in which each actor plays a character with the status level indicated by the card. Observers should then reflect on what status they believed the actors were playing. However, this is not a guessing game and performers should use the audience feedback to consider how they could communicate their status more effectively.

Changing status in a group

This is a whole-group exercise using the same pack of cards prepared for the last exercise. Each person takes two cards from the pack at random. One will represent the status their character is when they enter the improvisation, the other the status they will end up as (choose the order yourself). A scene in which a lot of people can interact is set up, such as a café, a doctor's waiting room or a railway station platform, with a couple of people in the scene at the start. Other members of the group must create a character to fit that environment, which they can enter and leave as the scene dictates. The status change can be sudden and attached to something that happens in the scene or it can be gradual, but it must be justified in terms of the character and the action.

Allow the scene plenty of time to get going. Often with a whole group exercise such as this, the scene only becomes natural and spontaneous when it has been playing for a good ten minutes and the actors have stopped trying to create 'interesting' things to do. If the scene starts to break down, reflect on why this happened and start again.

Group improvisation exercises

To practise improvisation, you can start with any kind of situation and build a scene up from it. You can find ideas by taking magazine or newspaper headlines or articles, looking at pictures, brainstorming for ideas around a theme, using characters or situations from a book, film, play or television programme or using one of the story creation exercises above.

The following exercises are designed to improve improvisation skills and, if they are repeated often, will help to improve creativity, confidence and trust within a group. For the exercises to work, all group members must be willing to jump in and join the scene without being pushed.

Action from physical images

Everybody stands in a space and freezes into any kind of pose they wish – standing, sitting, crouching, lying down, etc. Do not think about your pose too much or try to make it look like anything in particular. Use your whole body, including your arms, to create interesting shapes, but make sure you can hold the pose without wobbling or falling over. Each time the group leader calls 'change', change your pose instantly, making it as different from the last one as possible, and freeze. After a few changes, the group leader will pick two or three people to hold their poses while the others relax and move to the sides. On the word 'action', those still frozen will try to begin a scene, without hesitation or consultation, suggested by their poses and their positions relative to one another. Once the scene has played out, everyone gets back in position and the process starts again.

When the group becomes confident with this exercise, it can move on to the 'tag' version. One person strikes a series of poses, pausing with each for a few seconds. When someone else thinks of a scene suggested by one of these poses, they shout 'freeze' and then begin improvising the scene, which the first person has to follow. Repeat with a different person in the centre.

Image freeze tag

This exercise develops from the last. Two actors improvise a scene that revolves around a physical activity. When one of the spectators sees the actors in the scene assume a physical position that suggests a completely different scene, he or she shouts 'freeze', then 'tags' one of the actors and takes their place, starting a new scene from the same physical pose.

For instance, two actors may improvise a scene in which they are lifting heavy boxes onto a shelf. When they have their arms up in the air miming lifting the boxes, a third actor may freeze the action, tag one of the actors to take her place and turn the scene into an aerobics class. If the aerobics class includes some 'stepping', a fourth actor may freeze the action, replace one of the actors and turn it into a scene in which he is being chased by a gunman up flights of stairs.

Keep this exercise running if possible until everyone has been tagged several times. The scene should change completely each time; for instance do not just change the aerobics lesson into another type of exercise class.

Word freeze tag

This exercise is identical to the last, except that instead of freezing on an action the freeze is on a word. The new actor tagging in then starts a new scene from the same word.

Snowball

This is the same as the above two exercises but without the tag. Choose to base the exercise on either physical actions or words. When a word or action suggests another scene, someone shouts, 'freeze', joins the acting area without anyone stepping out and begins the new scene. The new actor should change the scene completely from whatever it was before.

Try to keep the group focused when there is a large number of people acting together. It is very easy for the scene to become chaotic, with everyone having their own little conversations without a proper focus for the audience in the scene.

Performing improvisation

Improvisation is a common and extremely useful tool for teaching performers and for rehearsing and it is a popular option in UK examinations. Most acting examination syllabuses contain an improvisation component. Candidates are usually examined on two different types of improvisation skills: spontaneous or instant improvisation and prepared or polished improvisation.

Spontaneous improvisation

This is true improvisation, as we defined it at the beginning of the chapter. The actors are given a stimulus to create a scene from and must begin the improvisation without any preparation or discussion. This may seem a daunting prospect at first, so actors may be given a short amount of thinking time until they are confident. Keep shortening the thinking time until no preparation time is given at all. If you use the exercises described above, you will already be performing spontaneous improvisations.

The following exercises are similar to those used in most improvisation examinations. Each starts with a specific stimulus, but similar suggestions can be provided by a group leader or by the group. If the stimulus is a word, phrase or situation, each person should write two or three suggestions on separate slips of paper, which are all folded, put into a pile together and picked out at random (remember when writing them that you may pick your own!). If it is an object, each person should bring in some objects and a way devised of picking at random who uses which one (perhaps by writing the names of the objects on slips of paper or giving each a number and drawing them out at random). Any of these exercises can result in solo, duo or group scenes. Occasionally use the same stimulus again and try to create a totally different scene from it.

Situations

Begin a scene from a given situation, such as:

- a blind date
- an argument between teenager and parent over how late they can stay out
- getting the wrong meal in a restaurant
- someone with an annoying habit sitting next to you on the bus
- giving someone some bad news.

Object

Create a scene that centres on a given object, such as:

- a map
- a traffic cone
- a mobile phone
- a snorkel
- a calculator

- a compass
- a TV remote control
- a newspaper.

Start line

Create a scene that starts with a given line, for example:

- Can you help me please?
- Did you really think you would get away with it?
- You'll never guess what (or who) I just saw!
- I think there's someone downstairs.
- Come on, we're going to be late.
- Did you hear something?
- Someone told me this place was haunted.

Note that although these are the first words spoken, there may be some action before the line is said.

End line

Create a scene that ends with a given sentence, such as:

- That's the last time I go anywhere with you!
- Did you see his face?
- This is not the end of this!
- I've never been so humiliated!
- I always thought you were the quiet one.
- Come on, let's go home.

The scene does not have to end when these last words are spoken.

Character

Create a scene based around a given central character, such as:

- an old homeless person
- a sharply-dressed businessman or woman
- Cinderella

- someone who is often picked on or bullied
- the Big Bad Wolf
- an obsessive fan of a pop star
- a wise old wizard.

Some of these characters may immediately suggest a story to you but, if not, try putting them in situations that are unfamiliar to them, such as putting the Big Bad Wolf in a school playground, or making the old homeless person a guest of the Queen. Also try the following variations on this exercise:

- Put two or more of these characters together and see what happens between them.
- Create a scene in which the chosen character is important but never appears.

Emotion

Create a scene around a given emotion, such as:

- love
- fear
- hatred
- anger
- boredom
- frustration
- happiness
- jealousy
- sadness.

Think about what could happen to arouse the most extreme form of the given emotion. Do not simply try to play the emotion; you must play the action that gives rise to the emotion for it to make sense as a scene.

Title

Create a scene from a given title, for example:

- The Gift
- The Kingdom Under the Sea

- A Holiday Nightmare
- The Stranger
- Lost in the City
- The Red Shoes.

Combination

Take two or more of the ideas from the previous exercises and combine them into one scene, such as the Big Bad Wolf, anger and a map, or a blind date, a traffic cone and a newspaper.

Prepared improvisation

The term *prepared improvisation* may seem to be an oxymoron (a term that contradicts itself) but it refers to a method of formulating ideas for a production using improvisation before polishing and rehearsing them for performance. This is more often referred to in theatre as a devised production; however, some examination boards define devised work and prepared improvisation slightly differently, so read the criteria carefully if you are devising an examination piece.

Your starting point may be a stimulus similar to those used for spontaneous improvisation, or you may be left to find your own ideas. Some groups begin with an issue they feel strongly about, such as drugs, abortion, prejudice, homelessness or the environment. While there is nothing wrong with tackling such issues, it is very easy to fall into the trap of preaching your views and not paying sufficient attention to the plot or the characters. Show characters that hold a different point of view to you arguing their case convincingly. To do this, you will have to research the subject carefully to find out what the counter-arguments are. Remember that if the piece is for an examination, each performer must have enough to do for the examiner to assess their performance.

Prepared improvisation exercises

- Use the spontaneous improvisation exercises above as stimuli for a prepared improvisation. A prepared piece should be longer with a more solid structure and better-defined characters and may require some research.
- Collect all the information you can from newspapers, television reports and the internet on a major current news item and devise a piece from it for performance.

Tutorial

Practice questions

1 What is meant by 'accepting' and 'blocking'?

2 Give examples of high and low status behaviour.

3 What is the difference between spontaneous improvisation and prepared improvisation?

4 For a devised piece you have been involved with, describe the process that you went through to create your final performance piece.

Seminar discussion

How do you think improvisation could be used when rehearsing a scripted play?

Study, revision and exam tips

1 Keep a notebook to record anything that you find interesting, such as overheard conversations, interesting news items, the characteristics or gestures of a person you have seen and how you felt when you were in a certain situation. Think about how you can use these notes to construct stories and characters.

2 Keep repeating improvisation exercises and inventing new ones; the only way to improve your skills is by practising.

Working with Scripts

Basic script work

It started with a script

Almost all drama on stage, on television and at the cinema is created from a script. It is the basic source of information for everyone involved in a production including actors, director, choreographer, designers and technicians. It is therefore essential that anyone working in or studying theatre knows how to read a playscript.

Why do I need to learn how to read a script? Why is it different from reading a book?

There is an enormous difference between reading a play and reading a novel. Some of the major differences are listed below (see if you can think of any more).

Novel	Script
Contains detailed descriptions of events, people and places to help the reader to imagine them.	Contains mostly dialogue, plus just enough extra information to tell us some of what the audience sees.
A complete, finished piece of work that anyone can pick up and experience.	The framework for a piece of work that is only complete when it is performed in front of an audience.
The reader can pause or turn back in the story at any point.	The spectator sees the whole play in one sitting and when each moment passes it is gone forever.
Reading is a private, solitary activity.	Theatre is a group social activity.

Although playscripts are often studied in English literature classes, they are not written to make sense on their own; their full meaning is only apparent when they are performed. Just as in normal conversation, the spoken word is only one of the ways in which the play communicates with its audiences. It is said that in normal conversation we derive only around 7 per cent of meaning from the words spoken, 38 per cent from the way those words are said and 55 per cent from body language. When we read a script we only have the words, so 93 per cent of the play's meaning is absent. To reclaim more of the meaning, we have to use some imagination.

Creating drama from a basic text

In the work on status, we used improvisation to investigate different interpretations of a simple piece of text. We will now use a similar exercise in order to create a whole scene from just a few spoken words.

Basic text exercise

Take a simple text such as:

1. Well
2. That's it
1. That's it
2. Great

or:

1. Yes
2. I can't
1. You have to
2. Yes

Split into pairs, with each pair taking one of these scripts (preferably not one written by them, so they have no preconceptions) and create scenes from the scripts. There must be no other dialogue apart from that in the script, and the lines cannot be changed, re-ordered, repeated or re-allocated. The dialogue can all be spoken in one block, or it can be divided up using pauses or action. Take some time to work on your scene, but *do not give it an ending.* When the scene is performed, you are not allowed to end it until the session leader tells you to stop – this could be after one minute or it could be after ten minutes.

After each scene, ask the spectators for their comments. Did the actors stick to the 'rules'? Did either of them look as though they wanted to speak at any point or did the silences look natural? Did the scene tend to fade out after the dialogue had finished or did they continue to act convincingly? Go back and work on the scene further, bearing in mind the comments made.

The point of this exercise is to demonstrate how much meaning is communicated by elements other than the words used. The scripts have very little meaning on the page, but by varying the way these words are said and the action that accompanies them they can be made to mean a lot of different things. Of course, most scripts give far more information than this, but just as much work has to be put into creating the physical world of the play in order to give it life and meaning.

> ### Text exercise – *Macbeth*
> In groups of three, stage the opening scene of *Macbeth* between the three witches. As in the above exercise, you cannot change, re-order, repeat or re-allocate any of the words. However, you can add pauses, action, effects, music, props, costumes, movement/dance, chanting, noises, make-up/masks, lighting, drumming or anything else you can think of to put across the evil, the magic and the danger in this short scene.

Play analysis

Dividing the action

Many plays are divided into acts and scenes either by the playwright or by script editors. Even where this is not the case, a play can be divided into digestible chunks to make it easier to analyse and rehearse. The great Russian director and acting teacher Konstantin Stanislavski used the example of a turkey being prepared for a meal. It is not possible to eat a whole turkey in one mouthful, so firstly it is carved into its separate pieces, such as legs, wings, etc. These parts are then carved further before being put onto the plates of the diners. Even these pieces are too large to be swallowed whole, so they are cut up with a knife and fork until the pieces are small enough to digest. The same is true of a play; to take a whole play and try to stage it all at once is far too daunting a task, but if we keep dividing the play into smaller and smaller segments, eventually we will have something that is small enough to work on in great detail. These smaller segments are reassembled at a later stage (unlike the turkey!).

Most experienced directors will do this automatically and instinctively, but to begin with it helps to have a system to follow. The system described below is based on Stanislavski's 'Method of Physical Actions' and Brecht's rehearsal methods as described in his Model Books. The methods for breaking down a script used by these two great directors later in their careers were very similar, although their intentions were different.

Breaking down your day

Write a list of everything you did from the moment you got up this morning. (A small tip: you may find it is easier to remember if you start with the most recent thing and work backwards.) You should end up with a list of general activities:

1. Got out of bed
2. Had a shower
3. Got ready to go out
4. Had breakfast
5. Went for bus.

Each of these activities could be a whole scene in a play or film about your day.

Image exercise 1

From each activity on your list, create a frozen image (or tableau) using the people in your group to represent the action. In other words you are creating a three-dimensional comic-strip version of your day by moulding the people in your group into a frozen, statue-like picture for each major event. (At this stage, you could draw the images as a comic strip if other people are not available to work with you.)

This is fine as an account of your day, but if someone wanted to be able to recreate these events by acting them out they would need much more information. Take one of your activities and break it down into more detailed events. For instance, we could take number five, 'Went for bus', and create from it the following list of events:

1. Left house
2. Went to bus stop

3. Waited for bus
4. Got on bus
5. Sat reading newspaper
6. Got off bus.

Image exercise 2

Now create another sequence of frozen images for your new list, just as for the last exercise. One of your images may be the same as the one you used for the episode you have just broken into events.

We are getting nearer to a sequence of things that can be acted out, but each of these headings is still too general for a detailed performance. Each event can now be separated into one or more actions that can be performed by an actor. For instance, 'Got on bus' may consist of:

1. Signalled for bus to stop
2. Got onto bus
3. Paid driver
4. Took change and ticket
5. Went upstairs
6. Found an empty seat near the back and sat down.

This is the process of breaking down a scene into actions that you can actually perform. The episode 'Went for bus' could be performed in many different ways and it is not clear what actually happened without more information. Even more detail could be added to this; for instance 'paid driver' could be expanded to 'Paid the driver who complained about me not having the right money and gave me back a load of small change'. You now have a list of playable actions that an actor could perform in this section of your 'play', even if they do not add up to a particularly gripping scene.

The following exercise is based on one created by German director and playwright Bertolt Brecht to try to get his actors to focus on the information they were delivering to their audience and to make it as clear and detailed as possible, rather than just trying to express emotion.

Street scene

On your way here today you witnessed a traffic accident in the street. Now tell the rest of the group the story of what happened to recreate the event vividly for them. Most people will tell a story about something they have seen using a combination of description, demonstration and mimicry (and often exaggeration) of the voices and gestures of the people involved, so you should do the same. Be as imaginative as you can with the events. Was there an argument? Did anyone get upset or angry? Did one of them try to run away? Did the bystanders get involved? Did the police arrive? If your spectators do not understand something, they should tell you so that you can explain it more clearly.

When doing this exercise, you are not trying to impress your spectators with your acting skills by showing 'real' emotion or 'becoming' the characters involved in the incident. You are simply trying to tell a story in the clearest way possible. This is the basis of what you are trying to do with every scene. You could take this scene (in fact why not try this as an exercise?) and stage it fully using different actors to play the different roles. However, if anything you add or change from the simple account of a witness above makes the story less clear, the alteration should be changed or removed.

Breaking down a whole play

We will now examine the process of breaking down a play in the same way that you broke down your day in the above exercises. For this you will need the script of a play you know reasonably well, preferably one you have read at least two or three times.

Many plays are already divided into acts and scenes, but some are not – or contain very long scenes that can be broken down into a number of distinct sections. Try to find where each complete section ends and the next starts – it may be at the end of a scene, where one or more characters enter or exit or where one major action ends and another begins. Give each section of the play a title that sums up the important action in as few words as possible.

For example, we could divide the first act of *Romeo and Juliet* into the following sections:

- Prince tells Capulets and Montagues to stop fighting on pain of death
- Romeo Montague reveals he is in love with Rosaline
- Lady Capulet tells Juliet she is betrothed to Paris
- Romeo and his friends go to the Capulet ball
- Romeo falls in love with Juliet at first sight.

The whole of the first act has been summarised in five short sentences. These do not follow the usual scene divisions, but these were introduced by editors and not put in by Shakespeare. Brecht's play *Mother Courage and her Children* is divided into 12 scenes. For his own production of the play in 1949 he gave each scene a title, beginning with:

1. The business woman Anna Fierling, known as Mother Courage, encounters the Swedish army.
2. Before the fortress of Walhof Mother Courage meets her brave son again.
3. Mother Courage switches from the Lutheran to the Catholic camp and loses her honest son Swiss Cheese.
4. The Song of the Grand Capitulation.
5. Mother Courage loses four officers' shirts and dumb Kattrin finds a baby.

And so on. Brecht has taken what he believes to be the most important element of each scene and summarised it in just a few words. (If you know the play, you will know that each scene has a title in the script different from those listed above. These were written for projection onto the stage to draw the audience's attention to the important themes and issues; the titles listed above were for the actors and director to get to the heart of the story.) *Mother Courage* is a series of episodes involving the title characters rather than a continuous story like *Romeo and Juliet*. Depending on the nature of the play you have chosen, you may have a series of sentences that tell a story, as for *Romeo and Juliet,* or a sequence of related episodes, as for *Mother Courage.* Either way, you should have a summary of the most important action in the play.

Scene title images

As you did with the summary of your day, take each scene title and create a frozen image to represent that title. Each image must be constructed from a detailed knowledge of the whole scene, not just of the moment it represents. Who is on stage at that moment? What are they thinking? Where are they looking? What expression is on each of their faces and bodies? Where is the focus of the scene – in other words where do you want to lead the audience to look (it does not have to be just one place)? How can changing the relative positions of people, set and props strengthen the relationships between the characters? Look back to the section on status in Chapter 2 to remind yourself how physical changes can drastically alter meaning. If the play depicts a time, place or situation you are not familiar with, you will need to do some research to create an accurate picture. Keep in mind where your audience is viewing the scene from and make sure they can see everything that is important for them to understand the meaning of the scene. Spend time on making each image as clear and detailed as possible. Someone walking into the room with no knowledge of the play should get a good idea of what is going on just from your frozen tableau.

If you complete this exercise properly you will have gained a reasonable understanding of how the story of the play works, but there is still a way to go...

Breaking down a scene

Just as you did with the breakdown of your day, the next stage is to break down each of your scene headings into a series of activities. For each activity, describe the action in a short sentence. You should use the least number of activities possible to tell the whole story of the scene. For instance, Act II Scene 2 of Frank Wedekind's play *Spring Awakening*, which could be given the title 'Wendla questions her mother about the facts of life', can be summarised as follows:

> *Frau Bergmann gives Wendla a basket to take to Wendla's sister Ina. She tells Wendla that Ina has had a baby. Wendla questions her about the stork bringing the baby. She frightens Frau Bergmann by threatening to ask the chimney sweep about the stork. She then makes up a story about a man in the street. Wendla tries to persuade Frau Bergmann to tell her where babies really come from. Frau Bergmann lies to her to 'protect' her from the truth. She then sends Wendla on her way with the basket for Ina.*

Here a whole scene has been summarised in just eight sentences, each of which represents a separate action. Similarly, Brecht summarised Scene 5 of *Mother Courage* in the following five sentences:

> *After a battle. Courage refuses to give the chaplain her officers' shirts to bandage wounded peasants. Kattrin threatens her mother. At the risk of her life Kattrin saves an infant. Courage laments the loss of her shirts and snatches a stolen coat away from a soldier who has stolen some schnapps, while Kattrin rocks the baby in her arms.*

The first sentence may not seem like an action, but Brecht must have thought it was important to establish to the audience that a battle has taken place before anything else happened. How can people and objects be arranged on the stage in order to show that a battle has just taken place? In filmmaking, this is known as an 'establishing shot', and many scenes benefit from giving the audience an initial image and time to take it in before a word is spoken. For instance, if a character is alone and the script says that someone else enters, it may aid the spectators' understanding of the situation if they are shown the first character's mood before the second character comes in.

Scene breakdown images

Take one of the scenes from your breakdown. It does not necessarily have to be the first scene in the play – sometimes it is better to start with a few key scenes and then fill the others in later. Your scene should already have a title and an image. Now describe the action of the scene in as few short sentences as you can without missing out anything important. This is where you may have to use some imagination, as you will need to expand on the information given in the script. Each sentence now becomes a title; create an image for each title. Again, spend time on the details of the image – not superfluous details merely for decoration but details that help to put over the story and the meaning to the audience. Once you think you have perfected your images:

1. Find the 'key image', the one that gives the scene its meaning and contains its most important action (this will probably be near the end and may very well be the one you chose for your scene image). Work on making this image more extremely funny, shocking, surprising, sad, chaotic or whatever the effect of that moment is intended to be on the audience. Work back through all of the images leading up to the key image to make the build-up more effective.

2. Show your images one by one as a 'slide show'. Hold each image absolutely motionless for at least five seconds and then move quickly to the next position, perhaps when someone claps. Go through this several times to get used to the sequence.

3. Choose a short section of dialogue – it may be one line, two lines or part of a line – to go with each image. Move into the image on the clap, then on the word 'action' animate the scene and speak the line, then freeze again until the next clap.

4. Write down all the action that will take place for each section of the scene. Do not be confined to scripted dialogue and stage directions, and be as detailed as

you can (you can change your plan later after you've tried it out to see whether it works). Go through the scene section by section, with each character performing the actions and telling the audience what they are doing, just as in the 'Street scene' exercise. Dialogue should be treated like any other action, and can be summarised to the audience ('Romeo told Benvolio that he was in love with Rosaline') or spoken like the dialogue in a book ("You can't really insist now that I'm 14 I still have to believe in the stork?" said Wendla').

This may seem like a lengthy process, but once you have completed this work you will have a physical map of the whole play. You will also have analysed how the play works, how the individual components contribute towards telling a story and how to put that story over to an audience. This process will help you to look at the scene as physical, visual action rather than as staged dialogue. What happens between the lines can often communicate more to an audience than what is said. If you have done this work well, you should find that the dialogue will fit naturally with the images you have created and you will probably find it easier to learn. You should remember that none of these details and images is set in stone and everything can be changed during later rehearsals if you find that something doesn't work or discover a better way. However, you should keep your notes from this early work so that you can look back and see whether later changes really have improved the play. If this is an examination piece, you may need these notes to write an essay or written examination, and may also have to submit them for marking.

Although the above is written as though you are rehearsing for a production, these exercises are also extremely useful if you are analysing a play or scene from a performance perspective to write about it (an analysis of a play for English literature would look at different aspects but some of this work could still be helpful). Even the most experienced directors will tell you that no matter what they work out beforehand on paper or in their heads, they never really know how, or if, something will work well until they try it out in the rehearsal room with real-life actors.

Creating a character

What is a character?

The actor's job is to take words on a page and create the character behind those words, which may be very different from the actor playing the role. Before we examine what 'character' actually is, try these exercises. Both are quite similar but often produce very different results.

These exercises produce characters that create an immediate visual impression to an audience, even though

Strings

The actors should walk around the room at random, not interacting with one another. The session leader calls out parts of the body, and everyone walks as though they are being pulled along gently by a piece of string attached to that part of the body (the string is being pulled hard enough for that part of the body to be prominent but not so that the person is dragged along). Afterwards, examine the types of characters that each part of the body implied. You will hopefully find that different people managed to get very different results from the same body part. For instance, a string attached to the belly button could produce characters who are fat, pregnant or feeling bloated or ill after eating or drinking too much.

Prominent parts

Again the group leader calls out parts of the body while everyone walks around the room. For this exercise, walk around as a character for whom that part of the body is the first thing people notice about them. Again examine the types of characters produced at the end. For instance a 'nose person' may be nosey, have a cold, have a large nose, be snobbish, scratch or twitch their nose a lot or be sniffing as though there is a strange smell.

they lack any real depth. However, they can be developed using further exercises. Choose one of the characters you have just created for the following exercise.

Hot-seating

Place a chair in the middle of the room: the 'hot seat'. Each person is asked to take the hot seat in turn, and they must sit on it *in character* and answer any question from other members of the group as they believe the character would answer. They cannot answer, 'I don't know' unless they believe that is how their character would answer. They may even believe that their character would answer, 'Mind your own business!' Do not just focus on what the character says; think about how they would speak, how they would sit, what mood they would be in, even how they would approach the chair and sit down.

It can be useful to repeat this exercise at different stages in the development of a character, as each time you will build on previous work and probably come up with something new. It is important that you analyse the results each time to assess what is relevant and useful. You may find that some things you have said are inconsistent with earlier work, in which case you need to decide which is more appropriate for the character. The following is a natural progression from this improvisation exercise to add more detail to your characterisation.

Character biography

Using the results of the previous exercises as a starting point, write a biography of your character. Include everything you can about them, for instance gender, social status, parents, friends, age, occupation, era, monetary status, religion, ethnicity, physical appearance, social skills, education, where they live and past experiences.

From a simple game, you have now created a character with many of the attributes of a real person. Your character may not be particularly 'realistic' – the 'Strings' and 'Prominent parts' exercises usually produce larger-than-life, cartoon-like characters – and much of what you have written may not come across to an audience, but it could inform the way your character reacts to situations that he or she comes across in the play. To develop from this work, you could start to create scenes in which some of these characters meet and interact.

To answer the question, 'What is character?', character is all of the things you have just listed. However you should remember that the audience can only interpret the character from what it sees and hears. Anything that the actor thinks or feels but does not show communicates nothing to an audience. This does not mean that everything has to be broad and obvious, but if you want the audience to understand something you must give them something that they can see or hear. If the physical actions of the character are chosen well and performed skilfully, the spectators will fill in the character's thoughts and feelings from their own imaginations.

Creating characters from text

Now we will apply this work to creating a character from a script. Take the script that you were analysing earlier in this chapter and select the character you are playing or studying.

1. Go through the script and make a note of everything indicated about your character by what your character says, what others say about him or her and the stage directions.
2. Research into the world of your character. This may include research into the time and place the play is set and written (they may be different), details about the character's education and occupation and so on – anything that could affect how the character speaks and behaves. These first two stages can be completed between receiving the script and beginning rehearsals so that you go into rehearsal armed with as much information as possible.

3. From this information, write a biography of your character. Be as detailed as you can, making up information wherever necessary to complete the picture, but make sure it is consistent with the information you have obtained from the script and your research (if your research appears to contradict the script, the information in the play takes precedence).

4. Hot-seat your character. Make notes of any useful details that come from the hot-seating and add them to your other notes.

5. Now try to create your character physically. How might he stand? How would she walk? What gestures or mannerisms might he use? How would she sit down? Experiment physically to see what works.

6. Take some general situations from the play – and maybe some that are not in the play – and improvise the scenes. Your character should act in ways that are consistent with the preparation work you have done.

7. Fit your character work in with the image work you have done on the scenes, changing any images that do not appear consistent with the way your character would behave. Look at the details of how your character behaves or reacts at every moment, even when not central to the action. Even when doing nothing, you should be doing nothing the way your character would.

Tutorial

Practice questions

1 From a play you have studied, choose one character and describe how you believe it should be played. Give details of voice, movement and other aspects of character.

2 From a play you have read, take a single scene and break it down into a sequence of activities. How does this breakdown help us to understand how the scene works?

Seminar discussion

How can background research help when putting together a production of a play and when and how should it be used?

Study, revision and exam tips

1 Read as many plays as you can of different types and try to imagine how you would stage each play and perform the characters.

2 When you see a play, try to get hold of the script and work out what choices the director and actors made in creating the production from the text. If you can see two different productions of the same play, examine the different choices made and how this affects the production.

3 Always keep notes of everything you do in preparation for a production as there could be some detail that will be valuable to you at a later stage when you may have forgotten it. These notes may also be necessary for revision or may have to be submitted for marking if this is an examination piece.

Designing the Stage

Designing a play involves more than simply creating a three-dimensional backdrop to the action. The actors interact with the design to create the meaning of a play and to communicate that meaning to an audience. A theatre designer therefore has to understand the practicalities of actors working on stage as well as how the actors and scenery work together to create a visual narrative.

This chapter will cover:
- designing for the theatre
- creating a design.

Designing for the theatre

What is theatre design?

Although the word 'designer' is now used for the person who creates the sound plan for a production, design is usually considered to be an arrangement of the visual. A designer creates something for us to see – posters, packaging, clothing, furniture, fabrics, wallpaper, websites and so on – to try to put over a specific visual message.

So what do we see in the theatre? The most obvious design element of a production is the stage set or scenery, which consists of various objects arranged on the stage to give an impression of the place, style and mood of the play. The lighting designer ensures that the actors can be seen, but can also use light, shadow and colour to suggest time, place and mood. Actors wear costumes and, sometimes, make-up designed to enhance their playing of the characters. There is one extra visual element that a designer for stage must always incorporate into designs that a painter, for instance, does not have to contend with: the actor.

A stage set makes a visual statement by itself, but as soon as an actor moves within it, the image the audience sees has changed. Very often, the way the actor moves within the stage set indicates to the audience where he or she is and how the location impacts on the character, the play and, ultimately, the audience. A stage designer does not create a fixed image but a constantly changing one, which is continually transformed by the actions performed within it by the actors. Where a painter creates a whole picture with a complete meaning, a set designer must leave part of the visual message untold for the actors and the action to complete the picture.

Completing the picture

This exercise demonstrates how the stage picture created by the set design is only completed when the actors move within it. Position a table in the acting area with a chair on each side of it. Act out the following scenes in pairs on this 'set'. Examine how exactly the same set can be used to create completely different scenes depending on how the actors move within the scenery.

1. First person is a manager sat behind a desk. Second person is an employee about to be fired for poor work.
2. First person is an employee sat in the manager's office. Second person is the manager returning to his or her office to fire the employee. (This may seem similar to the first example, but think about how the second person will enter the office differently if they are a manager in their own office rather than an employee. The actors not only show that this is an office, but whose office it is and who is in charge of whom. This relates to the work on status – a character can have a status relationship with a place as well as with another character.)

3. First person is man or woman cooking breakfast. Second person is their son or daughter (or husband or wife) coming in for breakfast and late for school or work.

4. First person is waiter in a restaurant, second is a diner waiting for someone to arrive who is late. (Again this is similar to the previous example, but will be acted differently to show a different place and mood.)

5. First person is a tour guide and second person a visitor in a stately home where the table and chairs are exhibits. A famous person once sat at this table many years ago.

6. First person is a sales person, second is a customer. Second person is buying a new dining table and chairs and cannot decide which one to buy.

7. Try to think of a few ideas of your own about how the same scenery could be used to create different scenes without them being used as anything other than a table and chairs.

But how does this relate to the real world of theatre productions? A stage set consists of more than just a table and chairs.

Firstly, this exercise demonstrates the principal that the designer should let the actors tell some of the story rather than give everything away with the set design. Secondly, for reasons of money, practicality or production style, the design *could* be as minimalist as this for a play. The National Theatre has its own workshops and scenery stores plus sophisticated machinery for moving it on and off stage, but a small theatre-in-education company performing at three or four different schools in a day would not have the time to put up and pull down a large set or the transport to move it (not to mention the money to pay for it) and it may not fit into some of the rooms in which they have to perform. Even when the money and facilities are available, a production style that uses the skills of the actors and the imagination of the audience to change location can be very powerful and satisfying for an audience and can permit complete changes of scene without any change of scenery.

Positions of actors

A director usually coordinates movements of the actors within the space, but many leading directors have very close associations with a particular designer. The designer creates a space that serves the play and the production and gives the director and the actors as much freedom as possible, but sometimes he or she will have much more involvement in the direction. German playwright and director Bertolt Brecht could not begin rehearsing a scene until his designer, Caspar Neher, had planned the arrangement of actors in the stage space. British director Peter Brook has designed many of his own productions so he has the flexibility to change the design during the long rehearsal period without having to refer to anyone else.

The way actors are arranged on a stage can say a lot about their situation and their relationship to one another before any of them speaks or moves. Try the following exercise to illustrate this.

Word images

Get into groups of about four or five people and give each group a word from the following list:

- play, home, hell, journey, fear, horror, life, boredom, happiness, waiting

Each group must then create a frozen image or tableau to represent that word using every member of their group. Do not forget to pay attention to facial expressions. Bear in mind, when you are creating the image, that you may have to hold it for some time.

When the images have been created, show them one at a time to the whole group. When viewing another group's image, walk around it to see it from every angle, then choose what you think is the best viewing angle and stand or sit there. There is no right or wrong answer to this so different people may choose different angles, but be prepared to justify your choice. From that position, point to, in your opinion:

1. the centre of focus of the image – in other words the point in the image that the viewer is most drawn to look at. There may be more than one. Why are you drawn particularly to look at this point? Perhaps the people in the image are looking or pointing at that place.
2. the people in the image with the highest and lowest status – look back at the work on status in Chapter 2. Give reasons for your answer.

Finally, try to give the image a name. This may have nothing to do with the original word. All of this should be completed without any assistance from the group showing its image. While they know what they intended to show by their image, it is very useful to listen to what an audience reads from it to see whether it could be made clearer next time. Sometimes an audience reads much more interesting meanings into a performance than the performers ever thought of!

This exercise will have given you some idea of how relative positions of actors to one another, the actors' eyelines and the spectators' viewing angle can affect how an audience reads a stage picture. If everyone looks at one person or object, the audience will tend to focus on this as well. If one person is physically higher than the others, this will often – although not always – give them a higher status. A moving stage image is considerably more complex as it is constantly changing, but it still needs to be constructed so that the audience is given a view that enables them to see all of the most important information. You may have been told that you should never turn your back to the audience because facial expressions are a very important way for an actor to communicate and the actor's speech will be heard more clearly if he or she is facing the audience. However, an actor with his or her back to the audience can be a powerful image – for example, if you wish to conceal what the character is thinking or feeling at that moment, to conceal their identity or to prevent the audience from seeing something about their face. Not being able to read someone's expression can be quite disturbing, which is why dark glasses that hide the eyes can give someone a higher status.

Setting actors' positions and moves for a scene is known as *blocking*. The director sometimes works this out in advance and teaches it to the actors, but it is often a more gradual process that evolves during rehearsals and is worked out between the director and the actors. There are some standard terms that refer to stage positions, which are illustrated in Fig. 4.

Note that stage left and right are from the point of view of the actor looking at the audience, so from the point of view of the audience and, usually, the lighting and sound operators, stage left is to the right and stage right to the left. Stage left and right are occasionally still referred to by the old names of *prompt* (P) and *opposite prompt* (OP) respectively, especially in old scripts, from the side that the prompt (the person who follows the script and feeds the actor a line when he or she forgets it) traditionally sat. The terms *upstage* and *downstage* come from the use of a rake, which is a slope on the stage that goes upwards away from the audience; an actor moving towards the back of a raked stage – or *upstage* – would therefore be walking uphill.

Some of these positions have traditional associations that it can be useful to play around with. The star of a show used

Fig. 4:
Stage positions

AUDIENCE		
downstage left	downstage centre	downstage right
centre left	centre stage	centre right
upstage left	upstage centre	upstage right

to always enter from up left, as this is the position that the eye of the spectator is drawn to most in the western world, apparently because in western society we read from left to right and from top to bottom. You can often still see this with solo singers, cabaret performers and star guests on chat shows. In mediaeval mystery plays, Heaven was stage right and Hell stage left – the word 'sinister' comes from the Latin *sinistra* meaning 'left' because of this. Especially in British pantomime, you may still see evil characters enter from down left and good characters from down right.

Position of scenic elements

As you have seen in the above exercises, a whole environment can be created with skilful acting and careful positioning of actors with little or no scenery. However, the style of the play and production may require something a little more elaborate. You need to consider some of the same things when positioning scenery as when positioning actors, such as making sure the audience can see what they need to see and focusing attention on the important elements of a picture.

Building up a scene

Following on from the last exercise, each group should think about what scenery they think they need to complete the scene. This could be used to create the impression of a real location, such as a room in a house, or something more abstract, such as Hell. You will not have to build this set so you can be as ambitious as you like! You can use walls, furniture, objects on the floor, objects hanging from the ceiling, platforms to create different levels, objects or designs painted on surfaces – let your imagination take you wherever it wants to go. Decide where your audience is going to view your scene from and make sure it can see everything it needs to see. Draw the scene on paper as it would appear from the front, and then draw a plan – a diagram of where everything and every actor is as though viewed from above. Finally, build a simple three-dimensional model of the set (card and balsa are commonly used for set models). Decorate the model as you would like the final, full-sized set to look. Do not forget to include scale models and cut-outs of the actors in the scene to show how they fit into the design and to give an idea of scale. Look at your model from the audience's angle and make sure that everything important is visible and that the effect you want has been achieved. You should then present your finished model to the other groups as though you were showing and describing it to the actors or production team of your play.

You should spend some time on this exercise, as it will give you a taste of the process that a set designer has to go through. You began with a scene and from that created designs and a model of a set, which could be used to create a full-sized set for a production. You have considered the positions of the actors and the viewpoint of the audience. The one thing you have not yet considered is the theatre itself.

Putting the design into the theatre

The set for a production fulfils two apparently opposite functions: to reveal and to conceal. It can reveal location, time of day, historical period, mood and maybe even something about the characters. It may also have to conceal actors waiting in the wings, the back and side walls of the stage and technical equipment (although some styles of design and production make a feature of exposing the technical equipment). It may also have to conceal something or somebody on stage that the audience should not see.

One of the major considerations when creating a design for a particular stage is the sight lines. These define the areas that can be seen by at least part of the audience as follows:

The above diagrams are for a proscenium theatre, but all theatres have their own characteristics when it comes to audience visibility and a designer must be aware of these. You will see above that the upstage left and right corners offer poor visibility for end seats close to the stage. To spectators on

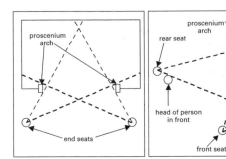

◀
**Fig. 5:
Sight lines in
plan and side
view**

the front row, the actors' legs and objects on the floor may be hidden by the stage; further back, the head of the person in front and the top of the proscenium arch may restrict the view of the lower and upper regions of the acting space. The extent of this effect depends on the slope of the auditorium and the height of the stage; a flat auditorium and no raised stage seriously restricts visibility for anyone not on the front row. A balcony may obscure the top of the proscenium opening for those underneath it. On the other hand, end seats may offer a very good view into the wings, and a front-row seat may have a good view of lighting equipment over the stage. One solution to this is a 'box set', which recreates the walls for three sides of a room and sometimes even a ceiling, but this can severely restrict positions for hanging lighting instruments. Flats – timber frames covered with painted canvas or hardboard – can be placed at regular intervals to block the view into the wings while still allowing actors to enter between them. These have to be carefully braced to prevent them falling over. Alternatives to flats are legs, which are strips of cloth, usually black, hung to create the same effect. These need to be weighted at the bottom to prevent movement when people walk past. The horizontal equivalents to legs are borders, which are strips of cloth hung across the stage to hide lighting instruments without getting in the way of their beams (spots of light on borders look messy and distract the audience's attention).

From this we can deduce that a good position for the main action is towards the front of the stage around the centre. This does not mean that all action and scenery has to be sited here,

Fig. 6:
Masking sides
and top of stage

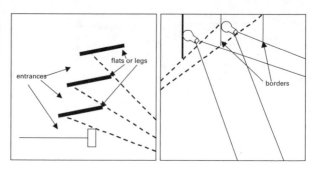

but you should be aware that if you place it elsewhere on the stage it might not be seen by everyone. End seats and rear seats are often sold at a cheaper price as 'restricted view'. There was a time not long ago when a number of theatres were built with regular seating that all had a fairly good view of most of the stage. However, to get the same number of seats in it was necessary to have a longer auditorium, and so some audience members were a long way from the stage and cut off from the action. Having some seats with restricted view at a cheaper ticket price makes it possible to have more seats closer to the stage, creating a more intimate atmosphere, and means that more people can afford to attend the theatre.

The above exercises have assumed that you are designing for an end stage. Having spectators on more than one side completely changes your sight lines and limits where you can place tall items of scenery.

Moving the audience

Take your design from the last exercise and think about how you would change it if the performance were to be:

1. on a thrust stage
2. in-the-round
3. on a traverse stage
4. a promenade production.

Most theatres rigidly separate the areas occupied by the audience and the performance. However, this does not have to be the case. The opening stage direction of John McGrath's play *Border Warfare* says, 'As the audience enter, not more than ten minutes before the start of the show, they are coming into the Forest of Scotland in the Dark Ages' and goes on to describe trees, stuffed animals, 'live' bears and a wolf that jump out at audience members and animal sounds that fill the theatre, not just the stage. Stephen Daldry's production of Arnold Wesker's *The Kitchen*, designed by Mark Thompson, built a large restaurant kitchen right out into the stalls from the stage that the audience looked down on from the balconies. Jerzy Grotowski's production of Christopher Marlowe's *Doctor Faustus* arranged long, narrow staging platforms like banqueting tables and sat the audience at them as though they were guests at a feast.

Bringing the audience into the design

Take the opening scene of *Macbeth* used in the previous chapter and create a set design for a completely empty room – in other words with no stage or fixed auditorium – that brings the spectators directly onto the spooky, magical heath as soon as they walk into the room. Think about how you would use lighting, sound effects, music and items of scenery to create a disturbing, sinister effect before the play even begins. How would you seat the audience – or would you leave them standing?

Creating a design

Script

Before attempting to create designs for a play, you must read the script a few times, studying every detail that may affect the design. Stage directions are likely to be your main source of information, but the dialogue may also contain important details about the scene (in Act I Scene 5 of *Macbeth* the King opens by saying, 'This castle hath a pleasant seat' – so we know we are in a castle). The dialogue will also indicate the mood of the scene, which may be reflected in the design. Make some preliminary notes and sketches, but do not do any detailed work until you have consulted the director and the rest of the production team to make sure that your ideas fit with the style of the production.

In an ideal world, the designer would attend rehearsals, creating and amending his or her designs as the production evolves to include new ideas. In the real world there is rarely the money and time for this, and most of the important decisions about the design have to be made before rehearsals commence so that the set builders can begin work. The model is often shown to the actors at the first rehearsal to show them the space they have to work with. The floor of the rehearsal room should be marked with tape to show where walls, doors and other objects will be placed. Temporary rehearsal props need to be found if the actual props are not available for rehearsals. These last two tasks are usually carried out by the stage management team, which liaises with all departments to provide everything needed at rehearsals as well as for performances.

Research

Whether your set is going to be a detailed recreation of an actual place or just a suggestion of it, you should know something about that type of environment in the real world, which may mean you have to do some research. This may involve looking through books or magazines or perhaps going out to visit some places, armed with a sketchbook and camera. If your play is set in a New York apartment, find magazines with pictures of them. You may even find an American estate agent's website with photographs on it. If the setting is a Victorian drawing room, search your local library for books with pictures of rooms, furniture and clothes from the period. You should always base your work on actual objects, locations or clothes rather than looking at other stage, television or film productions so that your designs are your own interpretations and not your versions of another designer's work.

Style

The search for a unified production style was the reason that the production designer's job was created. In a realistic production, a bookcase painted on a flat rather than an actual three-dimensional bookcase would look out of place. Some styles, such as pantomime, are better served by painted-on scenery and larger-than-life props that are nothing like the real objects they suggest. It must be remembered that this style must match the physical and vocal performances of the actors; a colourful clown speaking and acting like someone in *Eastenders* would be inconsistent. Theatrical style is more than just a choice of colours and materials; it affects every element of a production. Style can also bring out themes in a play more strongly; a play set in a single location, particularly if it is indoors, can reinforce a character's feelings of being trapped and unable to change their circumstances, whereas constant changes of location can indicate that change is possible. Darkness, lightning and witches emphasise the presence of evil in *Macbeth*.

Design elements

A scene design may use objects found in real life. However, even in a realistic production, some real objects may look out of place or not be visible enough to an audience. Other objects, such as brick walls and forests, would be impractical to use on stage if they were real. In a non-realistic style, every item will probably have to be created or adapted to fit in with the designer's overall concept. There are some standard items used for creating stage sets that any designer needs to be aware of.

Cloths

Cloths are large pieces of material hung in the stage area that may be plain but are often painted with anything from a simple design to a whole scene. *Backcloths* create a backdrop to a scene and may be painted with, for instance, a city skyline or a forest. *Cut cloths* give a limited three-dimensionality to a scene by cutting out areas of the cloth to allow something behind to show through, such as a tree cloth with the gaps between the branches cut out (do not forget that cloth branches will not hang upwards unless they are attached somewhere). A *cyc* (cyclorama) or *sky cloth* is a light-coloured backcloth that can be coloured with lighting or projected onto. A *gauze* is a special cloth that looks like a normal cloth if lit carefully from the front but which becomes almost invisible if a scene behind it is lit. This can be used to make something appear instantly or to fade gently from one scene into another like a dissolve in a film.

In larger theatres, cloths may be *flown*, which means they are lowered into view from a space above the stage known as a *fly tower*. Where this space is not available, they may be brought in on a *wipe bar*, a single curtain track across the stage, by pulling a rope. A cyc may be fixed in position for the whole performance.

Curtains

Tabs (tableau curtains) are brought in on a double rail from both sides so that they overlap in the middle. The *main tabs* are the main front curtains, often made of heavy velvet material, although these may be flown in large theatres. Many directors and designers consider tabs to be a bit old-fashioned, but they are still used in many theatres and can be useful to cover a (quiet!) scene change while another scene continues in front.

Flats

These have already been described when we looked at masking of sight lines, but their usefulness goes way beyond this. They can be banked together and painted to create walls and backdrops like those created by backcloths. The disadvantages of flats are that they are heavy and much more difficult to move quickly in a scene change and they have to

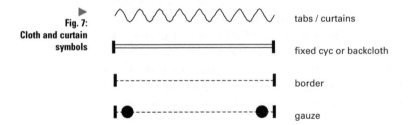

Fig. 7:
Cloth and curtain
symbols

tabs / curtains

fixed cyc or backcloth

border

gauze

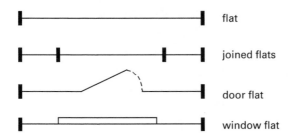

flat

joined flats

door flat

window flat

be firmly fixed to prevent them falling over. However, they can be grouped together in different ways to create different shapes, whereas a cloth can only be straight and flat. You can therefore create rooms with corners, alcoves, doorways and corridors. Also, whereas backcloths usually have to be hung parallel to the front of the stage, flats can create more interesting asymmetrical shapes. For instance, instead of creating a room with walls on the left, right and upstage sides of the stage, try using diagonal walls with the corners down left, down right and upstage off-centre.

Flats must be fixed securely, either by attaching them to the stage, walls or grid or by fixing braces to the back of them that are held down by heavy stage weights. *Book flats* are pairs of flats hinged together so that, provided they are set at an appropriate angle to one another, they are free-standing and reasonably secure. *Cut-outs* are shaped sections made from hardboard or plywood. These can be used in a similar way to cut cloths, but as they are made from wood they can be cut to more elaborate shapes without needing extra support. *Ground rows* are cut-out flats that sit low on the ground, used for such things as low walls, fences, grass and flowers.

Platforms and rostra

When you were creating images at the beginning of this chapter, you may have found that the more interesting pictures had people at different physical levels – perhaps some were standing, some sitting on chairs, some crouching and some on the floor. These levels can also contribute towards indicating the status relationships between characters. The set design can help to create levels by including platforms, rostra, steps and slopes. Remember that

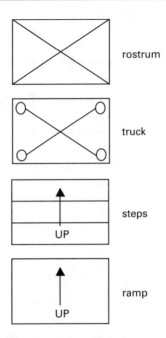

rostrum

truck

steps

ramp

introducing higher levels changes the sight lines. Canvas or carpeting on the tops of platforms can help deaden some of the noise from feet.

Trucks

Trucks are platforms of various sizes on wheels. They are sometimes used just as mobile platforms, but they are often set with scenery and props to enable a whole scene to appear and disappear very quickly. Some system of brakes or chocks must be used to prevent the truck from moving when someone steps on it.

Revolve

The *revolve* is a circular section of the stage floor that rotates. This can provide a very quick way of changing a complete scene, by merely rotating the stage to take the current scene out of view and reveal another. It can also give a sense of movement and is often used to signify a journey by the actors walking against the turn so that they are walking but remaining in the same place. A full-stage revolve is used effectively in this way in the popular musical of *Les Misérables*. The National Theatre's Olivier Theatre has a *drum revolve*, which not only rotates but also rises out of the floor to reveal different platforms and levels inside it.

Drawings

The stage plan is a crucial document on any production, as it will be used by almost every department. The director uses it to see where the actors can move. The stage management team uses it to mark out the rehearsal room and to plan the scene changes for the performances. The set builders, of course, use it to build the set. The lighting designer plans the positions and angles of lighting fixtures on a copy of the plan. It is therefore important that the drawing is accurate and to scale. A common scale for most theatres is 1:25 (4cm on the drawing represents 1m in real life), but very large theatres may require plans of 1:50 (2cm to 1m). Each scene must have its own drawing, although you can copy a basic template for each that shows the unchangeable items such as the stage size, borders, proscenium arch and so on. If you make any changes to your designs, you must inform stage management so that they can advise anyone else working on the production who may be affected. When you plan each scene, think about how the scenery can be changed from one scene into the next. A long scene change can seriously disrupt the pace of the show and leave you with a restless audience.

Tutorial

Practice questions

1. For a play you have seen, describe the concept of the set design and how it contributed towards putting over the story, characters and themes of the play.
2. For a performed piece that you designed set or costumes for, describe how you decided on your ideas for your designs and how they fitted in with the production as a whole and evaluate how effectively they achieved your aims in the final performance.

Student assignment

Read Shakespeare's *A Midsummer Night's Dream*. Pay particular attention to the two different worlds created by the play – the world of the mortals and the world of the fairies – and how they come together.

1. Research traditional stories and pictures of fairies and create designs for the play that utilise these familiar images.
2. Find a different approach to designing a magical world that may be more familiar to a modern audience. Where fairies were familiar to Shakespeare's audiences, a modern audience has different images of magic, such as outer space (the 1956 science-fiction film *Forbidden Planet* was based on Shakespeare's *The Tempest*) or unknown forces and conspiracies on earth (such as in *The X-Files* and *The Matrix*).

Study, revision and exam tips

1. Visit the theatre often, noting how set is used in each production and what effect it has. Keep a notebook of anything you particularly like or dislike.
2. Read as many scripts as you can and, for each one, sketch out some design ideas for a production of the play.

5 Lighting

One-minute overview

This chapter will help you to discover the basics of using light in a theatrical production. After some experiments and theory on the nature of light and colour, you will learn about the standard equipment used for theatre lighting and how to prepare to light a production.

This chapter will cover:
- lighting the actor
- lighting equipment
- designing the lighting.

Lighting in the theatre

Brief background

Lighting is a relatively new theatrical art form. At different times, performances have been lit by the sun, flaming torches, candles, oil lamps, gaslight and, more recently, electric light. When performances were all outdoors during the daytime, both actors and spectators were lit by the sun, but artificial lighting became necessary when plays were performed indoors. The introduction of gas lighting in the 19th century gave theatres some control over brightness levels in different areas of the stage. However, it was the flexibility, portability and controllability of the electric light source that allowed the establishment of lighting design as a distinct theatrical art form. Although the equipment used for stage lighting has changed considerably, the basic principles that we use today are pretty much the same as those devised by the earliest lighting designers in the late 19th century. However sophisticated the technology, a good knowledge of these basic principles is necessary in order to make the best use of the equipment available.

Safety note and assumptions

It is assumed for the purpose of this chapter that you have access to at least a basic lighting rig consisting of a lighting controller board, a dimmer unit and a number of lanterns. If you have no equipment installed, it is possible to hire quite cheaply a basic system consisting of a stand, some lanterns and a small dimmer unit that will plug into a standard 13-amp socket.

Electrical equipment should always be installed and regularly maintained by a qualified electrician, both for reasons of safety and to ensure that the circuits will be capable of carrying the large amount of electrical current required to power even a modest-sized lighting rig. Never plug anything into a socket that exceeds the socket's power rating; apart from the safety risk, you may find that you lose your whole lighting rig and maybe other equipment as well during a performance.

There are many other safety issues that may be relevant, such as working at heights, manual lifting and use of ladders and scaffolding. Please make sure you are aware of any health and safety requirements and recommendations applicable to the work you are doing. You should also be aware of any restrictions imposed on the building or room where you are working by the building's owners, the theatre licensing authorities, the local council or the fire service. If you are ever in doubt about any safety issue, ask. It is never worth the risk.

Lighting the actor

Positioning of stage lights

Stage lighting is, by its nature, a visual art and theories of lighting design make little sense unless one can see how the stage picture is affected. We will therefore begin by experimenting with light falling on the actor's face from different directions. For this you will need at least one powerful torch and a volunteer to be your subject (take it in turns so that everyone can see what the effects are). Try to get the room fairly dark, but it would be difficult to work in total darkness.

Lighting angles

1. Shine your brightest torch straight at the face of your subject from a few feet away. What effect does this have? The first effect will probably be to make your subject blink and squint in discomfort at having a light shining directly into their eyes, so they may wish to close their eyes for this first experiment. The features are well lit and the eyes can be seen to judge the actor's expression and mood. However, as everything is lit equally, there are no shadows to pick out the outlines of facial features, so it looks very flat and uninteresting. Also, if you look behind your actor, you will notice that a lot of light spills onto the walls and floor behind and he or she will have a large shadow. Ideally, your actors and scenery should be lit with different light sources to give you total control over the look of each and to make your actor stand out from your background, but in practice there is always some spillage.

2. Move the torch so that it shines straight down onto the actor's head. This gets rid of the large shadow and the light spillage, but what does it do to the facial features? They are no longer flat, but the eye sockets will be dark and the nose will look large with a long shadow under it. Apart from not being particularly flattering, it is not easy to read the facial expression, which is one of the actor's main tools for communicating to an audience.

3. Find a compromise between the last two positions that lights the actor's face so the expression can be read without flattening the features or spilling too much light onto the background. This should be at an angle of between 30° and 60°. If you only have a single light, this is a good position from which to light your actor.

4. Shine the torch up at the actor's face from the floor. What effect does this have? You will create some interesting dark shadows on the actor's face and a huge shadow behind them. While this angle is of little use in general lighting, it can be useful for some special effects.

5. Move the torch to the side of the actor. Now what can you see? You may see some of the facial expression, but the shape of the face is emphasised in an interesting way. There is also no shadow or light spillage on the back wall, so the attention is more focused on the shape of the actor's face and body. Side lighting is often used to light dancers, when it is usually more important to pick out body shapes from the background than to see facial expressions.

6. Move the torch to the angle from the vertical that you found in (3) and find the most interesting angle between side and front lighting. You will probably discover that, although the features are picked out nicely, the shadows on the face are very dark. These can be filled in by a second torch at a similar vertical angle to the first, but on the other side of the actor – around 90° from the first torch. If this second torch is less bright than the first or is a different colour, it will heighten the shadows without getting rid of them and will therefore avoid flattening the features of the face as in (1).

7. Shine the torch down onto the back of the actor's head. What is the effect from the front? Obviously this will not light any of the actor's facial features, but it creates an outline around the actor. By itself this is of little use unless you wish to show up the actor in silhouette, but in combination with other lighting it helps to pick the actor out from the background to give a more three-dimensional effect (this is commonly used in portrait photography, particularly on the hair). The angle of this light is not so critical, so it can be at a fairly steep angle to avoid casting long shadows or shining into the audience. If you have three torches, light your actor from the two front angles that you have just found in addition to this rear light. These are the main angles you will use to light an actor on a stage.

This is about as far as you can go with torches, as they do not offer much control over their light output other than 'on' or 'off'. With a small stage-lighting rig, set up three stage lights – it does not matter for now what types – so that the brightness of each can be controlled separately from three faders on a control board (you may need assistance with this). You can then experiment with altering the brightness of each light to see its effect. Try making each light in turn the brightest of the three to see how it changes the overall picture. Once you have experimented, try to balance the levels of the three lights to light up the actor's features without flattening the shape of the face or spilling too much light on the background.

The lighting for a scene will often suggest how light would fall in a similar situation in real life – although it needs to be much brighter to project this picture to an audience – and so in these cases you need to work out where light would be coming from. In real life, direct light comes from one or more sources such as the sun, windows or electric lights. Light is also reflected from walls, ceilings and other objects. Therefore the brightest light will come from the direction of the main lighting source and less bright, more diffused light will be reflected from other angles. Your main light, which you positioned in (6) above, represents the *main* or *key* lighting source, and your second or *fill* light and *backlight* represent the reflected light.

Light sources

Decide where you would position your main (key) light, fill light and backlight to light up an actor in the following scenes:

1. A large drawing room in the daytime with French windows upstage right and an imaginary window downstage.
2. A living room at night with one electric light in the middle of the ceiling.
3. A bright, sunny day in the forest.
4. Moonlight by the river (hint: reflections from water can be almost as bright as the main source but may not be stationary).

Position your actor at different points in the scene and try to work out where the direct and reflected light would be coming from. Draw a rough plan of the set and indicate with arrows the directions in which your three lights will shine.

Colour

So far, we have been working with unmodified white light, usually referred to as 'open white', but it is common to colour the beams of light. The colours could be chosen to look like realistic light sources; daylight may be more blue or yellow depending on the time of day, electric tungsten filament light bulbs give off a slightly yellow light and fluorescent strip-lighting gives a greenish cast. Colour can indicate time of day or weather, create a mood or feeling or just act as a design feature where realism is not required. Strong colours look interesting, but their light output is lower and they are of limited use in a realistic setting. Slight tints are more useful, as they allow enough light through to illuminate the subject and can be used to suggest how light falls in a natural setting while still creating a mood.

Colour is introduced into the light beam by slotting a frame containing coloured material known as *gel* onto the front of the lantern. Gel was originally made using animal gelatine, but is now manufactured in thin plastic sheets. It works using

**Fig. 10:
Gel frames
containing gels
(Rosco)**

colour subtraction, which means that whatever colours of light are directed at it, only certain colours can pass through. White light contains light of every visible colour, so shining white light through a blue gel will block everything but the blue light. Putting a blue gel in front of a spotlight will give you blue light, but it is important to understand precisely why that happens if you are going to start combining gels in front of the same beam. A primary blue filter will only allow primary blue light through, so if a primary green filter – which only allows primary green light through – is also put in front of it, all light will be blocked. Although it is possible to mix colours using more than one gel in a frame, it is better to find a single gel from the hundreds available that matches the colour you want. However, combining strips of gel alongside each other in the frame can create some interesting effects. The blocked light is turned into heat, which means that darker coloured gels tend to fade more quickly and eventually melt through (dichroic filters work by reflecting unwanted colours and therefore they do not have these heat problems, but they are rather too expensive for general use). Each gel manufacturer has a range of hundreds of colours and shades plus some special-purpose filters. They each produce swatchbooks containing samples of every filter they produce, which can be obtained from lighting suppliers and hire companies.

◄
Fig. 11:
Swatchbooks for two different ranges of gel colours produced by Rosco (Rosco)

Another way to mix colours is to shine lights of different colours onto the same spot. This is a method known as colour addition, as the colour produced is the result of adding all the different colours together. As white light can be split into the three primary colours (red, blue and green), shining primary red, blue and green light on the same spot will, in theory, produce white light. In practice it is very difficult to create 'pure' primary colours. Colour addition is often used to change the colour of a cyc cloth by using two or three groups of lights, each covering the whole of the cyc and gelled to a different colour. By varying the levels of each of the groups, the operator can mix different colours on the cyc and smoothly fade between them.

Lighting a coloured object involves colour subtraction. An object will appear primary red if it reflects red light and absorbs green and blue light. If this red object is lit with red or white light it will appear red; if lit with green or blue light it will, in theory, reflect nothing and appear black. It is therefore important that the lighting designer knows what colours are to be used for the set, props, costumes and make-up before deciding on which gel colours to use. Lighter tints of gels, as opposed to strong colours, contain some of every colour and are therefore a safer bet for general lighting. Another thing to bear in mind is that tungsten filament lamps are at their whitest when at full brightness, becoming more yellow as they are dimmed down, which will affect the colour of most gels. This can be an advantage, as it effectively increases the colour palette; dimming the levels of certain lights could be enough to introduce some 'warmth' into the scene.

Investigating gel colours

Get hold of a gel manufacturer's swatchbook and a small torch. Just looking at the colours of the gels does not give a real impression of the colour of light they produce. In a darkened room, shine the torch through different colours of gels onto a light-coloured surface or someone's face. Make a note of colours that you feel will be useful as:

1. daylight
2. artificial light
3. warm colours

4. cool colours
5. sinister colours
6. cheerful colours
7. colours that you like.

Adding colour

Take each of the situations you used in the 'Light sources' exercise above and decide what combination of colours you think you should use in each. Also choose colours that you could use in:

1. fairy story-land
2. the witch's castle
3. a treasure cave
4. hell.

Gobos

Gobos are used to shape the light beam. They are either cut from metal or printed onto heat-resistant glass and inserted into a focused profile spot in order to project an image. These

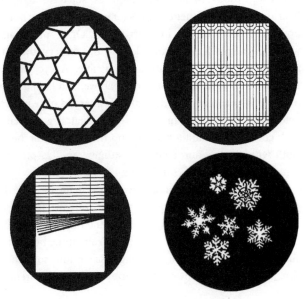

◀
Fig. 12:
A selection of
metal gobos
(Rosco)

images could be abstract patterns, a picture to act as projected scenery on a cyc (such as a New York skyline), an image of where the light is supposed to be coming from (such as a window) or a break-up pattern, which scatters the light beam like the sun shining between tree branches. A break-up gobo can give an interesting texture to the light that changes as the actor moves through it. Metal gobos create silhouettes, but glass gobos may contain colour and it is now possible to use them to project photographic images.

Lighting objects

Similar principles apply to lighting scenery and objects as to lighting actors. Use angles to explore and colour shadows and textures and to produce an interesting, three-dimensional picture. Remember where your main light sources are, as it would look a little odd if the sun on your set was coming from a different direction to that on your actors. Painted backcloths may look better lit flat as angled light may show up seams in the cloth and lumps in the paint. You would normally wish to control the level of light on the set separately from that on the actors so you can create a balance to make your actors stand out from the scenery. This requires separate lighting instruments and dimmer channels for each, which may not be possible if equipment is in short supply. On a small stage, where the actors are working close to the scenery, the spill may make effective separation impossible. A cyc can be coloured with lighting as mentioned above, and fading from one colour to another can dramatically alter the stage picture before the eyes of the audience. Traditional stage curtains look good when side-lit, showing up the folds in the heavy cloth with shadow and colour. Costumes can also produce some interesting shadows if lit from certain directions.

One type of cloth that deserves special mention is the gauze, which appears opaque when lit from the front, but becomes semi-transparent when the scene behind is lit. This can be a very effective way of revealing something before the audience's eyes, or of transforming a scene into something else. The scene in front of the gauze has to be lit carefully, preferably with side and top lighting, as light hitting the gauze directly will shine through and light up the scene behind.

Lighting equipment

Now you have experimented with different effects with light, we will have a look at the equipment used to create these effects in the theatre.

Lanterns

This is the name usually given to stage lighting instruments. A lantern, at its simplest, consists of a lamp (the equivalent of a domestic light bulb) and a reflector enclosed in a metal case. Many lanterns also have a lens or system of lenses and adjustment controls. Here are a few common types of lantern.

Profile

The profile has a high light output and its beam is focused with a clear lens. The focus can be controlled in order to give a hard or soft edge to the beam and shutters – usually four, on each of the four sides – can be used to close down and shape the beam. An iris can be inserted behind the lens, which has a lever to control the size of the beam at a particular focus. As the beam can be focused, images can be projected using gobos. A zoom profile is more complex, with a double-lens system that can be adjusted to a hard focus at different beam sizes. The profile is commonly used as the main lighting source and also for 'specials', as it is easy to control the spread of light.

Fresnel

The lens of the Fresnel (pronounced fre-NEL) has a stepped appearance – originally developed for use in lighthouses – which has the effect of giving a soft light with a wide spread. Its wide spread makes it ideal for giving a general 'wash' to the stage area, the soft edge making it easy to blend the beams of a number of Fresnel spots together. However, it has a tendency to spill light outside its main beam. The spread of light is usually controlled by *barn doors*: four hinged metal flaps on a unit that fits on the front of the lantern. Moving these flaps inwards reduces the spread while retaining the soft edge to the light beam. There is also an external control on the lantern to vary the spread of the beam by changing the distance between the lamp and the reflector.

An alternative to the Fresnel for soft lighting is the PC spot, which has a similar lens to a profile but is frosted to diffuse the beam. A similar effect can be achieved by using a diffusion filter in the gel frame of a profile to soften the beam, and some filters also stretch the beam out along one axis. There will probably be samples of diffusion filters in your gel swatchbook – try putting the filter in front of your torch beam and removing it to see how it changes the light. Also try rotating the filter in front of the torch to see whether it spreads the beam in a certain direction.

Flood

The flood is a much simpler type of lantern, consisting of a long, narrow lamp set inside a reflector tray. There are no lenses or adjustments and the only way to vary the spread of light is to vary the distance between the lantern and the subject, although it is occasionally fitted with barn doors to give some limited control. It provides a wash of light over a large area and is often used to light backcloths and cycs.

Parcan

This lantern is a narrow metal tube containing a par lamp with a built-in parabolic (hence 'par') reflector that produces a bright, narrow, oval beam of light. The parabolic mirror sends the rays of light out parallel to one another rather than spreading them out as in most lanterns, so the beam remains the same size irrespective of how far away the lamp is from its subject. It is often used in rock concert lighting, but is fairly common in theatre. With some smoke, the beams of parcans show as bright bars of light, and when banked together they can produce an effect known as a 'light curtain', which appears as a solid wall of light.

Follow spot

This is often a type of profile on a stand with additional controls and a cartridge on the front for flipping different-coloured gels in front of the beam. The operator moves the lantern to follow a performer around the stage. The beamlight (a parcan is a type of beamlight) is sometimes used as a follow spot; this gives a more subtle emphasis to its subject with a softer edge and it has the advantage of having the same size of beam however far away the subject is.

Intelligent lighting

Intelligent lighting is used extensively in the rock concert arena and in nightclubs and is becoming increasingly common in theatre. The instruments themselves vary enormously in the functions they offer, but they may be able to move, change colour, change gobos, focus, change beam size or create effects such as strobe (flashing on and off quickly), diffusion or rotating images, all under the control of the lighting desk. One intelligent fixture commonly used in theatre is a colour scroller, which fits on to the front of a normal lantern and allows the operator to change the colour of the light from the lighting desk. This can save having a number of sets of lanterns of different colours focused on the same area. Modern scrollers can change to a different colour very quickly and – which is probably more important in the theatre – reasonably quietly.

Lighting control

In order to control and alter the levels of light from each lantern, we need dimmer units to vary the amount of electricity sent to each lantern or group of lanterns and a console for the operator to control the dimmers from a convenient location.

Dimmers

Before it can be operated from the lighting desk, each lantern must be connected to a dimmer unit, either directly or via the theatre's internal wiring. A dimmer unit is split into separate channels; each channel can control one or more lighting fixtures up to a maximum power – for instance a 1,000W dimmer channel could power a 1,000W parcan, or two 500W floods, or a single 750W profile. Overloading a channel will cause the fuse to fail and the channel will become inoperative. If more than one lantern is plugged into the same channel, they will all operate together, so lanterns that need to be controlled separately must be connected to different channels.

Basic manual board operation

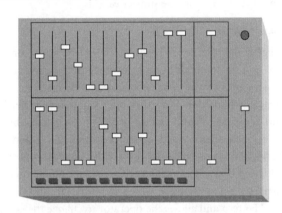

A manual lighting board consists of a number of faders, each of which corresponds to a dimmer channel. Pushing the fader up to the top will bring the lamp up to full brightness and pulling it to the bottom will turn it off. There is also a master fader to control the overall level of all of the channels. Bringing the master fader down will cause all of the lanterns to dim and eventually go off, creating a *blackout*. In this way, a scene can be set up on the individual faders with different lamps at different intensities, and the master fader can bring the whole lighting state up and down in a single, smooth action.

A development from this most basic board is a two-preset lighting controller. This board has two sets of faders operating the same channels, each with its own master fader. This allows the operator to have one scene 'live' on one preset while setting up the next scene on the other preset with its master fader down. A smooth *crossfade* can be achieved by bringing one master fader down and the other up at the same time.

Some boards make this easier by having the two preset masters side by side, one with 'full' at the top and 'off' at the bottom and the other with 'off' at the top and 'full' at the bottom. It is therefore possible to crossfade with one hand by pushing both faders together. It is usually preferable to lead with the incoming fader to prevent a lighting 'dip' in the middle. A flash button is often available on each channel which, when pressed, instantly brings that channel up to full, or to the level of a separate flash master, until the button is released. Some boards have a fade-time control, which allows you to set the time of a crossfade from a fraction of a second to several minutes, or other facilities to increase the amount of control and range of options for the operator. Even when there are separate masters for each preset and perhaps other functions as well, there will still be a *grand master* to control the overall output from the desk.

Basic memory board operation

A memory board can hold the levels of one or more channels and fade time in a single scene memory, so that the whole lighting state, from a single lantern to a complex pattern involving many different lanterns, can be brought up in a single action. Hybrid boards have a combination of channel faders and memory operation, and some desks have submaster faders that can be programmed to bring up a channel or groups of channels with a single fader.

Another facility provided by most memory boards is the ability to record a sequence of lighting changes called a chase. Each step of the sequence is programmed as a complete lighting state and, when run, the chase steps through them in order at a pre-programmed speed either once, a specified number of times or continuously repeating until told to stop. A chase can be used to create flashing light sequences for dance routines, flickering fire effects or subtle changes in lighting during a scene.

Modern memory boards are extremely sophisticated, with the ability to control dimmers, intelligent lighting instruments, strobe lights, smoke machines and even pyrotechnics (stage fireworks).

Designing the lighting

Your first basic design

Now we need to put all of this information together, combine it with our observations and imaginations and paint a picture with light.

The experiments you have done in the above exercises have enabled you to create a basic lighting state for a stationary actor. This would be fine if you only had to light one actor who never moved, but this is unlikely to be the case. As soon as the actor takes a few steps to one side, your carefully calculated angles are all wrong, if the actor is in the light at all. You therefore have to use enough lanterns from each direction to keep your actor lit from an acceptable angle in all the areas where he or she is likely to be. Using barn doors on Fresnels and shutters on profiles, any light that is at a poor angle or that spills onto scenery and borders can be cut off. At the points where the beams meet, they should cross just enough to prevent a dip in the light level but not so much that there is a bright spot. On an evenly lit stage, an actor should be able to walk across the stage and not become darker or lighter or change colour at any point.

One way to do this is to divide your stage into areas and to allocate a set of lanterns to each area. This method also gives you the opportunity to highlight some areas of the stage more than others. If you just need to generally wash the whole stage, you could divide it into squares but, if action takes place in certain areas that have to be separately lit, these will need their own sets of lanterns. Even in a naturalistic play with just a general cover of lighting, subtle, barely noticeable changes in the levels of different parts of the stage can focus the audience's attention on a particular area or character.

Remember when you are pointing and focusing the lanterns that your areas define where an actor can stand and still be fully lit; if you just light those areas on the stage floor, there will be parts where only their feet will be visible. It is useful to have a spare person to stand where the actors will be so that you can focus lights on them instead of guessing. If some areas of the stage have to be lit in different colours at different times, you will need a different set of lanterns for each colour (unless you have colour scrollers). However, you could save on equipment by using pale, neutral colours from the front and using top and side lighting to vary the overall colour.

The following is a simple solution to providing general cover. The stage is divided into six equal areas. Six profiles on the advance bar (the one over the audience) pair up to light the front three areas and six profiles on the first bar over the stage pair up to light the back three areas. Three Fresnels on the upstage bar each provide back lighting for two areas.

Fig. 14:
A simple lighting configuration
▼

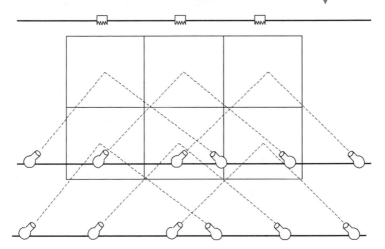

Designing a play

As with every other element of a production, lighting design begins with the script. Your lighting must serve the requirements of the script and the production. Make notes about everything that may affect the lighting, including locations of scenes, time of day, mood, entrances and exits of characters where lighting may change, references in the script to the light or colour and points in the script where one character or group of characters needs to be highlighted. Think about the general mood of each scene and how you can enhance this with the use of light and colour. Before you develop your ideas too far, you should discuss them with the director to make sure that they fit in with the overall concept of the production and to find out where the actors will be on the stage. Close liaison with set and costume designers is important for planning where your lighting will be able to go (there is no use planning side lighting for a box set) and what colours will work. Try to get samples of materials and colours that the set and costume designers plan to use and shine your torch through different gel colours in your swatchbook onto the material to see how it is affected.

Begin by marking on a copy of the set plan every position in which you can hang a lantern and plug one in. Divide your stage into areas, but bear in mind any point in the production where only one part of the stage is lit and make sure this is a separate area. Then you can start to build your design by placing lanterns on the plan in the positions and approximate angles you require them. The above symbols are commonly used for different types of lanterns, but any symbols will work as long as you provide a key. Also mark on your plan which channel the lantern is connected to and which colour gel is to be inserted into it. Gel colours are often indicated by numbers inside the lantern symbol (each gel manufacturer has its own numbering system). Channels are indicated by a number next to the lanterm symbol.

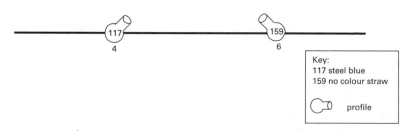

Key:
117 steel blue
159 no colour straw

profile

Fig. 15:
Indication of
colours and
channel numbers

During the performance, the lighting operator will usually work from a list of numbered cues (detailing exactly what action to take on each cue) and will be told when to bring in each cue by a member of the stage management team who is 'on the book'. It is much easier to have someone dedicated to cueing all of the technical operators from one master script than to have each of them try to follow a script and operate their equipment at the same time.

The form the cue list takes depends on the type of lighting board being used. The following is an example of a cue list for a manual, two-preset lighting board. On each row, the top number is the channel number and the bottom number indicates the level of the channel from one to ten.

Production Example production   Sheet 2 of 27

LX: 4   Preset: top   Action: blackout then up   Cue: Dennis enters

1	2	3	4	5	6	7	8	9	10	11	12	13	14	15	16	17	18	19	20	21	22	23	24
5				5	7	8			10		10			10					8				

LX: 5   Preset: bottom   Action: 10 sec cross   Cue: 'I think I'd better go'

1	2	3	4	5	6	7	8	9	10	11	12	13	14	15	16	17	18	19	20	21	22	23	24
						8	10	10	10		10			10		6			9				

LX: 6   Preset: top   Action: quick cross   Cue: All exit

1	2	3	4	5	6	7	8	9	10	11	12	13	14	15	16	17	18	19	20	21	22	23	24
					4		4	4						10									

Fig. 16:
Example cue list for manual lighting desk

The next example is less complex as it is for a very simple memory board. Instead of having to specify the level of each channel, we can just indicate the number of the memory which has all of these levels programmed into it.

Production Example production   Sheet 2 of 15

LX	Mem	Cue	Action	Time
4	6	Dennis enters	Blackout then up	5s
5	7	'I think I'd better go'	Cross	10s
6	10	All exit	Cross	1s
7	8	On gun shot	Snap	–

Fig. 17:
Example cue list for basic memory board

A more sophisticated memory desk may not require a cue list at all, as the screen shows a list of cues all programmed sequentially and the operator simply has to press the 'go' button when given the cue.

Tutorial

Practice questions

1 For a play you have studied:
- Describe your ideas for lighting one section or scene from the play using sketches and diagrams where necessary.
- Give details of precisely what your designs are intended to communicate to an audience, such as mood, location, time of day and period.

2 List the different types of stage lantern you know about and describe what each is useful for.

Student Assignment

Work with a group that is putting together a scripted or prepared improvised piece. Create a lighting design in collaboration with the others involved in the production and implement it.

Study, revision and exam tips

1 Visit the theatre often and note how lighting is used in each production and what effect it has. Keep a notebook of anything you particularly like or dislike.

2 Read as many scripts as you can and make notes on how you would light a production of the play.

3 When you are lighting a play, try to visit actual locations similar to those depicted and make notes on light sources and colours.

4 Contact a local theatre and ask whether they organise backstage tours. If not, ask them if they will let you speak to the lighting technicians and see the equipment they use.

6 Sound

One-minute overview

This chapter will look at how sound is used in the theatre and explore different ways of creating and using it during a performance. You will experiment with creating sounds before exploring the equipment used for sound recording and sound reinforcement.

This chapter will cover:
■ sound in the theatre
■ creating sound effects
■ sound reinforcement
■ creating a sound design.

Sound in the theatre

Sound is a feature of every performance and always has been. Even silent mime acts traditionally have music playing behind them, as a performance in total silence feels quite odd – perhaps even disturbing. From the voices of the actors to music and effects; from the laughter and applause of the audience to the person with the noisy sweet wrappers, every sound contributes to the experience that the audience has in the theatre. Just as a conductor controls the tempo and relative sound levels of the different instruments in the orchestra, the sound elements of a performance have to be balanced to create the effect required and allow the most important sounds to be heard clearly.

Actors are trained to use their voices to reach the back row of a large auditorium while appearing to speak almost normally. In the past, theatres were designed so that sound from the stage carried to the furthest seats. If you visit the huge outdoor theatre at Epidaurus in Greece, which was built nearly

2,500 years ago to hold around 20,000 spectators the guide will drop a pin in the centre of the orchestra to show that it can be heard from the highest tier of seating.

Music has always played an important part in the theatre and sound effects have always been used. The 'sound designer', however, is a relative newcomer to the theatre, arising from the increasing use of electrically amplified sound. Modern technology allows some very sophisticated use of recorded effects and amplification of sounds, voices and musical instruments, but the sound designer must work with all the other elements of a production to help create an appropriate style. This may be a loud, rock-concert sound for a modern rock musical such as *Tommy* or *Rent*, or it may simply be a few background sounds such as birds or traffic and the occasional door knock and telephone ring.

Creating sound effects

Live sound effects

The following is an exercise used in improvised comedy that demonstrates how live sound can be effective in a scene.

Vocal effects

One person improvises a scene in mime that would involve a lot of different sounds in real life, such as making a meal in a kitchen (taps, mixers, kettle, scraping toast, sizzling bacon, etc.) or fixing a car (car engine, wipers, car failing to start, car alarm, door and bonnet slams, steam from radiator). A second person creates all of the sounds *only with their voice* as the other person acts out the scene. This is a spontaneous improvisation exercise, so there should be no planning or collaboration between the performers beforehand. Although it may seem that the person performing the actions is in control of the scene, the person performing the sounds can also change the direction of the scene. For instance, the actor can decide to turn the key in the car ignition but the sound person decides whether or not the car starts!

Although this is an improvised comedy exercise, live sound effects such as these can be extremely effective in performance, as long as the style of the performance allows for it. Of course, in a normal performance there is no need to limit ourselves just to vocal effects; various objects can be utilised to create sounds that suggest something else. For instance, a gunshot can be created quite effectively by hinging together two pieces of wood and slamming the two halves together.

DIY sound-effects kit

You are now going to create your own do-it-yourself sound-effects kit. The effects you create now could be used in actual productions. For this exercise, you cannot use any recorded sound and everything you use must be transportable. In other words, you cannot use anything fixed in the room such as shelves, doors, windows or large items of furniture. You can use any objects, acoustic musical instruments (not electronic keyboards) and voices. Try creating the following sounds, and then add some of your own:

- Footsteps (on different types of surface such as concrete, grass, gravel)
- Door slam (different types of door)
- Wind (gentle breeze, howling wind, eerie wind)
- Rain (different amounts from drizzle to downpour, indoors and outdoors, on different types of surface)
- Thunder
- Door creak
- A crackling wood fire (think about what kind of material can produce a similar sound; there is no need to set fire to anything to create this noise)
- Door knocker
- Doorbell
- Horses trotting (on grass and on concrete).

Keep notes of exactly how you achieved each effect so you can use them in the future.

Some of the effects you have created here may need to be recorded and amplified to be useful in a performance, but they will probably all be useable. Although most sound effects are now recorded, certain sounds are more effective when created live. For instance, no recording medium can yet reproduce the speed at which the sound of a gunshot reaches its very high volume, and a recorded gunshot sounds 'softened' in comparison with the real thing. For a telephone ring, a device is used to ring the bell in the telephone on stage as it sounds more authentic than a recorded effect and it stops as soon as the actor picks up the receiver – which may not happen as realistically if the sound operator has to press a 'stop' button. If the telephone ring is essential to the plot, it is always a good idea to have a recorded ring as a backup in cast the ringer does not work or the telephone plug is kicked out.

Many methods have been used to create live sound effects in the past. Thunder was once created by rolling a cannonball down a wooden chute. A more convenient method was to hang up a flexible metal sheet and shake it. The sound of horses' hooves has traditionally been created using halved coconut shells or wooden blocks banged together. A wind machine was created by stretching a piece of canvas tightly over a drum using a weight, so that when the drum was rotated with a handle it rubbed against the canvas and made a 'whooshing' noise. Rain can be created by fixing wooden pegs through a sealed cylinder containing dried peas and tipping it slowly, or by dropping rice or lentils onto a reverberant surface. Sharply shaking a wooden tray filled with dried peas or gravel from side to side can recreate the sound of footsteps on gravel. For a door slam, a miniature door can be made – complete with locks, chains and a frame – that produces the same sound that a full-sized door makes. For fire, try rustling Cellophane. With some imagination you can create a wide range of sounds with very little equipment. For one production, a recording engineer came up with a very effective sound of a train slamming on its brakes by scraping a fork on a dinner plate.

Adding sound effects to a scene

Take a short section of a film or television programme on video and play it back with the sound turned off. Try to recreate all of the sounds that the scene suggests – your sounds don't have to be the same as the original. Use anything from your new sound-effects kit, vocal effects or anything else you can come up with. Practise adding the effects as the video plays back. When you are ready, 'perform' it for others to watch.

Recorded sound

Usually in modern theatre, most of the sound effects will be recorded and played back through loudspeakers at the appropriate time. The sound operator can therefore control all of the effects and hear how they sound to the audience without needing a range of devices and objects with which to create the sounds. These can be single sound effects or sounds that run in the background while a scene is played. Of course, these recordings have to be made first. To do this, you can use any of the methods you have already tried or you can go out and record actual sounds. You can also use commercially recorded sound-effects tapes and CDs, which you can find in larger record shops, but using recordings made by someone else is nowhere near as satisfying as using those you have made yourself.

Recording effects

Get hold of a portable cassette or Minidisc recorder. Go out and record some background sounds, such as a busy street, railway station, shopping centre, airport lounge, supermarket, café, club or quiet place in the countryside. Make sure you record enough of each sound to last the length of a scene – it is preferable to have too much recorded and have to fade it out than for it to cut out in the middle of a scene.

Now that you have some sounds, you can see how they can transform a scene.

Background effects

In groups of two or three, take one of the background effects you have recorded (or one from a sound-effects CD) and create a scene to perform with that sound running in the background. Make sure that the levels between the recorded effect and the performers' voices are balanced so that the audience can hear what is being said, even if you have to have the sounds quieter than they would be in real life.

Another thing to consider when using recorded sound effects is where the sound is coming from. A stereo sound system offers a crude way of positioning sounds by varying how much of the sound goes to each of the right and left speakers. Sometimes an effect can be enhanced considerably if the sound actually comes from the object that is supposed to be creating it. Small speakers can be placed near – or even inside – radio and television sets. A speaker near to a baby's pram can play sounds that the baby is supposed to be making. Speakers behind the scenery can play sounds coming from outside the room. A production of *Mrs Warren's Profession* at the Royal Exchange Theatre in Manchester positioned small loudspeakers in a flower bed playing sounds of insects, and the same theatre's production of *Kes* made the sound of the kestrel seem to fly all around the theatre. Certain types of atmospheric effects, or sounds designed to disturb or frighten the audience, can be striking if played through speakers in the auditorium, as used to good effect in the West End production of Susan Hill's ghost story *The Woman In Black*.

Recording formats

There is a variety of different media available for recording and playback of sound and new ones are appearing all the time. The following are those you are most likely to come across.

Vinyl records – These were used live for sound effects, background sounds and music, but the relatively poor sound quality and the difficulty of cueing a recording accurately make this a difficult format to use in a live situation. If you must use sounds from vinyl recordings for a performance, you should transfer them to another format before using them.

Reel-to-reel tape – This was the most common playback format for a long time, as the quality is good and the positions of individual sounds could be marked with coloured leader tape so that they could be easily found. However, the tapes are large and editing is fiddly, involving cutting the tape with a razor blade and sticking the individual pieces together with splicing tape.

Cassette tape – Cassettes are a more convenient size than reel-to-reel tapes, but the quality is not as good and it is very difficult to cue them accurately to the beginning of a sound. If you have to use cassettes, you should try to use a different cassette for each sound and cue them all before the start of the performance.

Digital audio tape (DAT) – These very small tapes can record a large amount of digitally recorded sound; they have been used for a long time for creating master recordings in recording studios. The quality of the recording is slightly higher than a normal CD recording but, as it is a tape, it takes time for the machine to wind between sounds, unlike CD and Minidisc, although the wind speed is considerably faster than cassette. Another drawback of tape is that it cannot start at full speed instantly. Some high-end DAT players get around this by storing a section of the recording in RAM, which is played back instantly when 'play' is pressed to give the tape time to get up to speed.

Digital compact cassette (DCC) – This was a digital version of the humble cassette tape developed by Philips, which has now all but disappeared from the market. It offers digital recording on a double-sided tape similar to a normal cassette and the machines can also be used to play back (but not record to) normal analogue cassettes. To fit the information onto the tape, it uses data compression to remove all sounds that the human ear cannot consciously hear. Moving to the next tape cue can be slow, the same speed as analogue cassette, and is not always accurate. However, this format offers cheap, digital-quality recording that is perfectly adequate for background sounds that do not need to begin instantly on a cue.

Compact disc (CD) – For a long time it was only possible to play back from CDs, but now it is possible to record onto CD-R (recordable) and CD-RW (rewritable). CD-Rs can only be recorded onto once, but they can be played back on most modern CD players. CD-RWs can be changed after recording, but they can only be played back on certain machines. CD offers high-quality digital recording on a disc that allows random access (in other words you can jump to any point on the disc almost immediately) and can be cued accurately to start instantly. Another advantage of CD-Rs is that they are extremely cheap, especially if bought in bulk, now that they are in common use for both audio recording and computer data storage. CD-Rs can record a maximum of 80 minutes of audio data on one disc. However, it is now possible to cram considerably more than this onto a disc using the compressed MP3 format, although only specialist CD players can currently play them back.

Minidisc (MD) – Although produced as a domestic format, it is in live performance that the Minidisc has really taken off, running the recorded sound for performances ranging from local pub acts to West End theatres. It provides almost instant random access and high-quality digital recording on a disc smaller than a CD but with a similar recording capacity. Tracks can quickly and easily be named, moved, divided, joined or deleted, with a few limitations, on even the cheapest domestic MD recorder. The 'auto pause' facility on most Minidisc machines can be used to play back just a single track and then pause at the beginning of the next track until you press 'play' again. This is extremely useful in live performance.

Digital versatile disc (DVD) – A DVD is the same size and shape as a CD but can hold considerably more information on two sides or separate layers of the disc. Despite difficulties caused by different recordable DVD formats from competing manufacturers, DVD is taking off as a recording medium for video and computer data (pre-recorded DVD has already almost replaced VHS tapes and is becoming a common medium for computer software). DVD audio has yet to establish itself, but it certainly has some potential for the future.

Hard disks and computers – The amazing success of Apple's iPod has brought the hard-drive music player (although the iPod is much more than this) into the consumer market in a big way. However, the stand-alone hard-drive recorder (one that is not part of a computer) has been used in recording studios for many years for recording digital audio. Computers have been standard tools in the studio since before hard disks were fitted to home computers. Initially they were mainly used as MIDI sequencers to record and play back sequences of signals to electronic musical instruments. The much higher speed, capacity and processing power of today's computers makes it possible to record, edit, process, apply effects to and mix down many separate tracks of audio information all inside the computer – something that, ten years ago, could only have been achieved by using a rack of equipment. For most sound designers, the computer is a very useful tool for editing sound before recording it to a different medium. However, computer-controlled systems are available for running the sound for theatre and theme parks. If you use a computer for theatre sound, you should invest in a sound card or USB or Firewire input-output unit with professional input and output sockets, as the mini stereo jacks used in standard sound cards do not offer sufficient quality for professional audio.

Multi-track recording

You should now have a number of sounds that you can use individually, but what if you wish to combine some of them? Maybe you could really do with having an announcement and a few more trains arriving and departing on that railway station background recording, or perhaps you could combine an outdoor crowd with a few fireworks to create a firework display, or add a few claps of thunder to that rain sound. You could do this during the performance by having multiple playback machines and starting each at the appropriate time (which you will still need to do if some of the sounds in the mix have to appear on a specific cue, such as a clap of thunder on a particular line of dialogue). A much easier method is to combine all of these sounds into a single recording by using *multi-track* recording.

You may not realise that your humble cassette recorder is actually a multi-track machine. For a recording in mono (short for monaural or monophonic), only one set of sound information needs to be recorded as an identical sound comes from every speaker. For stereo (stereophonic) recording, two sets of information are needed for right and left channels, as a stereo recording varies how much of a sound appears in the right and left speakers to fool the brain into believing that it is coming from somewhere between the speakers. A stereo recording machine is sometimes known as a 'two-track', and some live mixing desks have an output labelled 'two-track' to enable a recording to be made of a live performance. You could make a simple two-track mono recording by recording different sounds from the right and left inputs of a stereo recorder and then playing it back through a mono system. The balance control will dictate how much of each sound is heard.

Two-track recording

Try to create a thunderstorm using a rain effect and some thunderclaps using a cassette recorder. The simplest way would be to have two sound-effects CDs, one with the rain effect and one with the thunder effect, and connect each to one of the inputs of a cassette recorder (just use one output from each CD player). Start to record and set the rain effect running, then punch in thunder claps from the other CD as often as you want. If you play this back on a stereo system, put both speakers together and alter the balance control on the amplifier to control how loud the rain and thunder are relative to one another.

A stereo, or two-track, cassette tape actually has four tracks, as each cassette has two tracks on side A and two on side B, recorded side by side along the magnetic tape. The simplest dedicated cassette multi-track machines can record on all four of these tracks in the same direction, doubling the number of sounds you can record at one time. Of course, you can only record on one side of the cassette, as if it is turned over the same four tracks will be recorded in reverse. (This can be used for some special effects by recording things backwards, but remember that when you turn the cassette over, the track numbers are reversed, so that something recorded on track one will now be on track four.) The most useful additional facility on a dedicated multi-track machine is the ability to record on just one track without affecting the recordings on any of the other tracks. This means you can record just your rain on track one and then, while listening back to your recording, record thunderclaps wherever you want on track two without erasing your first recording. You can have as many goes as you wish at getting your thunder in the correct place without having to re-record the rain each time. You could also add, for example, a dog barking on track three and a car arriving on track four.

For this example, a recording could be produced fairly quickly without much preparation, but for a more complex mix it helps to have a plan. The following example is a possible plan for the rain effect described above.

Tape Count	Track 1	Track 2	Track 3	Track 4
000	Rain			
002		Thunder		
004		Thunder		
005			Dog bark	
007		Thunder		Car arrives, engine off
012		Rain		
014	Rain ends		Dog bark	
015				Car ends
016	Thunder			
017				Car door
018				Car door
019			Dog bark	
021	Thunder			
024	Thunder			
028		Rain ends		

◄
Fig. 18:
Example plan for four-track recording

You will notice from this plan that the rain effect ends at 014 on track one as it is not as long as the sound effect needed in this case; it is introduced on track two just before it ends on track one, so that the effect is continuous. You may have to adjust the levels at the crossover point to get the best join. If, when you come to record the effects, your times are not exactly the same as those on your plan, alter the plan. Then, when you come to do the *mixdown* – this is when you play back all of the tracks at once and record the results onto a conventional two-track machine – you know when to change the level of a track or other settings such as pan, EQ and so on (see later in this chapter). If you require more than four tracks, most machines allow you to 'bounce' down two or three tracks onto one spare track so that you can reuse the originals, but remember that once you do this you can no longer change the original tracks that make up this mix and each time you re-record there will be some loss of quality.

A four-track cassette recorder is the simplest dedicated multi-track machine you are likely to come across, but it is possible to make very effective and reasonably complex effects with some planning and imagination. Eight-track cassette machines can be used if you need extra tracks, and four- and eight-track Minidisc multi-track machines are now available at a relatively reasonable price. They offer digital-quality recording, little or no loss in quality when tracks are copied or bounced as well as processing only available with digital audio. Hard-disk recorders are now being produced at prices attractive to the home studio, often packaged with a digital mixing desk. These can record multiple tracks onto a computer hard disk and offer an impressive range of facilities, including sound processing and effects, random access, moving and copying of tracks and recording of 'virtual' tracks, which can hold a number of attempts at recording a track to enable you to pick the best. The major disadvantage of hard-disk-based systems is that the hard disk can be filled and backing up and storage of tracks on the disk may be difficult and slow.

Mixing sounds

Plan how you would recreate the following using a four-track recorder and a selection of sound sources:

- A train crash
- Summer in the forest
- A busy street in the city
- A restaurant kitchen.

If you have access to a multi-track system, have a go at recording these and the thunderstorm example used above.

Sound reinforcement

System overview

Sound reinforcement is the name given both to the use of amplified sound in a live environment and to the equipment used, although the equipment is also often referred to as a PA (public address) system. A typical system will look something like Fig. 19. This diagram could represent the heart of any system from that of a pub or club band to a stadium rock concert.

Microphones and loudspeakers

At opposite ends of the chain, we have two electro-mechanical devices that are very similar in design but have opposite functions. A microphone is designed to turn sound vibrations in the air into electrical impulses; a loudspeaker turns electrical signals from the amplifier into vibrations in the air, which we interpret as sound.

Fig. 19:
Diagram of a
typical sound
system
▼

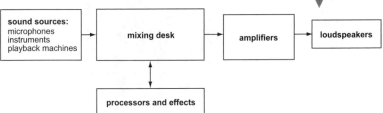

Microphones

A microphone is a mechanical 'ear' and different microphones use different methods of picking up sound signals. A dynamic microphone picks up vibrations with a diaphragm attached to a coil of wire in a magnetic field, and movement of the coil in the field induces an alternating current in the wire. A condenser microphone measures the changing capacitance between a fixed, charged electrode and an electrode made to vibrate by the sound entering it. Dynamic microphones are cheaper and more rugged and so tend to be commonly used in live situations. Condenser microphones are more delicate and need a source of power to charge the electrode, but give a more even sound at a wide range of frequencies and so are used extensively in recording studios.

Microphones have a number of different names, which describe the shape of the area around a microphone where it is most sensitive, or its *pickup pattern*:

a. **Omnidirectional** – picks up sounds equally well from all sides.

b. **Cardioid** – picks up sound mostly from the front. Gets its name from its heart-shaped pickup pattern. The tone of the sound tends to change with distance, which is why some singers hold the microphone right up to their mouths to take advantage of the additional bass the 'proximity effect' gives them.

c. **Hypercardioid** or **supercardioid** – a version of the cardioid with a narrower range at the front and a small

▶
Fig. 20:
A selection of
dynamic and
condenser
microphones
(Shure)

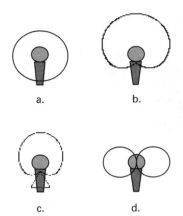

◀
Fig. 21:
Microphone
pickup patterns

a.   b.

c.   d.

amount of pickup at the rear. The narrower front pickup means that less spill from sounds coming from the sides enters the microphone.

d. **Bi-directional** or **figure-of-eight** – picks up from the front and rear of the capsule, which is mounted sideways in the microphone body to pick up sound from the two sides.

Radio microphones

Radio microphones use a radio signal to replace the cable between the microphone and the mixing desk, and so give the performer more freedom of movement. They are expensive to buy or hire, they use up expensive, high-powered batteries very quickly and they are more susceptible to interference (including radio stations or the radios of local taxi firms) and lost signal than wired microphones. Many of them also require purchase of a licence. However, they provide a way of close-miking a performer without any trailing cables, allowing them complete freedom of movement. The microphone is attached to a small transmitter, which may be built into the body of the microphone or be in a separate belt-pack, and its signal is transmitted via an aerial to a receiver connected to the mixing desk.

Lavalier microphones, which have very small microphone heads that can either be clipped to clothing or, preferably, attached to the performer's face, usually in the hairline on the forehead, are very common in theatre productions. These

Fig. 22:
Hand-held radio
mic, belt-pack
transmitter and
receiver (Shure)

Fig. 23:
Lavalier and
headset mics
(Shure)

can be concealed with hair and make-up so they are almost invisible. Headset microphones are now becoming more common, particularly in modern rock musicals such as *Rent*, where the visibility of the technology is part of the design concept. These are worn on the head like a headband and have a microphone extending in front of the mouth. Hand-held radio mics may also be used if their visibility is acceptable for the production.

Loudspeakers

In a speaker driver, the current from the amplifier passes through a coil of wire in a magnetic field, causing it to vibrate. The coil is attached to a cone to amplify the sound and radiate it outwards. A speaker cabinet will often contain more than one speaker driver so that each one can be specially designed to handle a certain range of frequencies. The tweeter is the smallest speaker, designed to handle the highest frequencies, and is designed to vibrate at very high speeds. The woofer is the largest speaker and it deals with the lowest frequencies. There may be one or more mid-range speakers as well.

If a speaker driver is fed frequencies outside its range, it will try to reproduce them. This will result in a 'muddying' of the overall sound and may even damage the drivers. A

◄
Fig. 24:
A pair of
full-range PA
speakers (Shure)

device called a 'crossover' splits the signal into its different frequencies and sends to each speaker driver only the frequencies it can handle efficiently. A passive crossover will sit in the speaker cabinet and handle all of this without the operator needing to intrude. An active crossover enables the operator to send different parts of the signal to different amplifiers and speaker systems in a large PA system.

The main PA speakers would normally be positioned between the performers and the audience (although see previous note about positioned sound effects). For the performers, the sound from the PA is very dull through the back of the speaker cabinet. They will also hear the sound bouncing from the back, wall of the auditorium after a slight delay, which can make it very difficult for singers and dancers to stay in time and tune. The solution to this is to use monitor (or foldback) speakers, which face the performers and enable them to hear what they need in order to perform properly. This is not necessarily the same mix as the audience is hearing.

Feedback

Feedback occurs when a microphone picks up the output of the speakers and sends it back through the PA to be amplified and sent out through the speakers again, creating a loop. This loop builds up and up and is usually heard as a whistle or whine that gets gradually louder (the frequency at which the feedback is heard depends on a number of things, including the characteristics of the room). The immediate remedy is to reduce the level of the offending microphone until the noise stops, but there are precautions that can be taken to reduce the likelihood of feedback occurring.

The first thing to do is to ensure that only microphones that are being used at any particular moment are *open* (turned up on the desk). The more open microphones you have, the higher the chances of feedback occurring. Secondly, make sure that all microphones are facing away from any speakers that their signal is being sent to. The ideal relationship between a microphone and a monitor speaker depends on the pickup pattern of the microphone: a cardioid should be facing away from the speaker but, as a hypercardioid has some rear pickup, it needs to be angled at around 45 degrees so that the speaker is in the microphone's 'dead spot'.

The instinctive reaction of many performers when feedback occurs is to cover the microphone with a hand, which changes the directional characteristics of the microphone and usually makes the feedback much worse. The best thing for a performer to do is to move away from the speakers. Also watch for performers with microphones suddenly moving towards each other. The sudden rise in volume (caused by the performers being picked up by one another's microphone as well as their own) can cause feedback.

The mixing desk

The mixer is the heart of the sound system. It can be a few knobs built into an amplifier or an array of knobs and faders that would strike fear into the heart of an aircraft pilot. Although the facilities may vary, the basic operating principles are the same from a small portable desk to a big studio. The following are the major features on most desks.

Master section

Here you will find either one master fader or one each for the left and right outputs to control the overall sound level leaving the main outputs of the desk.

Fig. 25:
Small and large
mixing desks,
showing a
similar layout of
controls (Shure)

Channel strips

As with a lighting desk, each channel fader represents a different device. There are a number of other controls associated with each channel:

Input level/gain/trim – This controls how much of the signal from the device enters the desk.

Auxiliary sends – These send part of the signal to a send output on the desk; turning the control varies the amount of signal sent from that channel. This may be used to send a signal to an effects processor, in order to add an effect such as reverb or echo to a sound before returning to the desk via another channel or a *return* input. It can also be used to create a different mix for foldback. Note that a *post-fade* send level alters in proportion to the position of the channel fader as well as the send control, whereas a *pre-fade* send works the same wherever the channel fader is positioned.

EQ – This stands for *equalisation*; it splits the sound into bands of frequencies so that the operator can adjust the tone of the sound. Shelving EQ is used to adjust everything above or below a certain frequency. In the mid-range, there may be controls that affect fixed bands of frequencies, or there may be a sweepable mid that allows you to choose which band of frequencies to adjust. Rarely, there may be a parametric EQ, which gives controls for frequency, cut or boost and the range of frequencies (or 'Q') that are affected. There may also be a bass cut switch to cut everything below a certain frequency, which is useful for microphone channels to reduce popping, wind noise and microphone handling noise.

Pan – This controls whether the sound from this channel is directed more to the left, right or centre of the stereo sound field. It can also be used to direct the signal to a sub-mix fader so that a group of channels can be controlled together or sent to a different output.

Mute/solo – Mute stops all output from the channel from entering the mix. This allows you to set the proper output levels for all of your input devices and mute them, only un-muting them when they are needed. Solo sends the signal from just that channel to headphones or monitor speakers so that the operator can monitor it on its own.

Fader – This controls the overall level of the channel entering the mix. By varying the fader levels of the different channels you can balance the sounds with one another to obtain the best overall mix of sound.

Gain structure

It is essential to get the sound levels correct at every point in the chain between source and speakers in order to obtain the clearest possible sound. Every signal contains noise, and the more the sound has to be amplified to obtain the required level, the more the noise is amplified with it. Therefore, if your levels are too low early in the chain, the signal will have to be amplified later on to compensate and noise will be added. However, if the levels are higher than the circuitry can handle – known as 'peaking' – the result is distortion, which at best sounds worse than the noise you are trying to get rid of and at worst can cause damage to components, particularly speaker drivers. Therefore each signal should be set to hit peak level without distortion when it is at its loudest on the whole of its path from the input gain of the desk right through to the input levels of the amplifiers (each mixing desk has its own method of setting optimum input levels, so you should consult the manual). This balance of levels throughout the signal path is known as the gain structure.

Experimenting with sounds

Connect a tape or CD player to a mixing desk (which is connected to an amplifier and speakers) by plugging it in to either a stereo channel or two mono channels. Set the input gain to the optimum level and then experiment with different settings of EQ and pan to see what the effect is.

Connect a microphone to a mono channel and set the input gain. Experiment with different settings while someone speaks or sings through the microphone as above. Connect up an effects unit by plugging an auxiliary send output to the input of the unit and the outputs of the unit to a return input. Make sure the level for the return is up and experiment with different effects settings on the unit and different send levels on the microphone channel. Write down any effects you like or think may be useful in the future.

Creating a sound design

Analysing the script

After all this experimenting with sounds and equipment, you will have some idea of what is possible in theatre sound. However, when you are designing sound for a production, the first place to go to is to the script. Make a note of every door knock, telephone ring, car arrival, clap of thunder, sound of a television or radio or anything that could become part of the sound picture. Look at where you can put atmospheric background effects such as traffic noise, birdsong or an echo on a stage microphone to give the impression of a castle or cavern – although remember it is possible to overdo such effects. Also note where music will come, if it is being used, and liaise with the composer if this is to be specially written. Look at which sounds can be live and which recorded and start to work out what equipment you will need and where it will have to be placed. Once you have some ideas you can discuss them with the director and see whether they fit in with

Cue No	Cue	Action
5	Lights up	MD track 1 to sub 1 & 2
6	Tony enters	Fade sub 1 & 2 out
7	Sally 'No more peanuts!'	MD track 2 to main outs, un-mute ch 2 & 3
8	End of song	Mute ch 2 & 3

Production Example production   Sheet 2 of 15

Fig. 26: his or her concept before you spend time and money on
Example sound developing them further.
cue list

Creating cue lists

Like the lighting operator, the sound operator will normally
work from a list of cues and be given 'stand by' and 'go' cues
by the deputy stage manager or whoever is 'on the book'.

Fig. 26 is an example of a cue sheet for a sound operator.

Tutorial

Practice questions

1 For a play you have studied:

- Describe your ideas for a sound design that would
  be suitable for a section of this play. Use diagrams
  or sketches if it will aid your explanation.
- What does your design communicate to an audience
  (atmosphere, location, time, mood and so on) and
  how does this fit in with the themes of the play?

2 List the different types of controls found on most
sound-mixing desks and describe their functions.

Student assignment

Get hold of a decent-quality recorder and record and
catalogue as many sounds as you can – maybe look at
the sounds on a general sound-effects CD and try to
create your own versions of them. These will then be
yours to use whenever you need them in the future.

Study, revision and exam tips

1 Listen to how sound and music are used in plays, films and television programmes and keep notes on anything that you find useful or inspiring.

2 Read as many scripts as you can and work out how you would design sound for a production of each play.

3 Contact a local theatre and see if they organise backstage tours. If not, ask them if they will let you speak to the sound technicians and see the equipment they use.

7 Writing about Theatre

One-minute overview

Anyone who studies drama formally will probably have to write about the subject at some time. Even those who do not will benefit from learning how to record their thoughts and ideas about theatre. This chapter takes you through the skills involved in writing about drama you create yourself and drama that you watch others perform. This chapter will cover:

- why write about theatre?
- analysing performance
- watching a play
- writing an essay.

Why write about theatre?

Throughout this book, theatre has been described as a practical subject. Why do we have to write about it?

As with any other subject, writing our knowledge down is a way of demonstrating to ourselves and to others that we know and understand what we have learned. This is what we are usually required to do for an examination or a marked essay. More importantly, the act of writing something down also forces us to investigate our thoughts further, making us think beyond what we have simply seen and been told. A play in performance is a complex union of many different elements, from the language, structure and content of the play text and its social, political, moral and performative implications to the technical and artistic skills of acting, directing, lighting, sound and set design. Analysing a production can help us to understand how the play works in performance as opposed to on the page. We can look at the various choices that were made for this production and compare them to our own ideas of what the play is about and how this can be communicated to an audience. This analysis of production is extremely useful to us when formulating our own ideas about what our ideal theatre can be – ideas that we can put into practice in our own productions. Analysis of our own work is an essential skill to master, so that we can develop the more effective elements and change or discard the less effective ones. This is a process we go through during rehearsals in order to keep improving the piece we are working on, but we can also examine our final performances in the same way in order to learn from them for the future.

In a wider context, the best published theatre criticism can help audiences by pointing out what they might miss or not fully understand the relevance of, and can help the art form by celebrating high quality and innovation and revealing deficiencies and areas for improvement. Of course, all criticism is only one person's opinion and can be disregarded or argued against. The ephemeral nature of theatre (in other words the fact that it only lasts for a moment and then is gone forever – even another performance of the same production will be always slightly different) means that written records are one of the few ways of preserving performances for future generations.

Analysing performance

From exercises to performance

If you have taken part in the activities in this book, you will have created some pieces of drama. However, you will probably have been missing one vital ingredient to make your experiments in drama into theatrical performances: an audience. However polished your moves and speeches have become during rehearsals, the presence of an audience, observing and responding to your work, changes your work into a performance, giving it new meanings and a reason for existing. We will now add this vital ingredient to the work you have been doing and investigate its effect.

Creating a performance for an audience

Split into two or more groups and give each group a different area in which to work so that they are not aware of each other's preparation processes. Each group should create a ten to 15-minute piece of drama; either it can be based on one of the exercises you have done previously or it can be completely new. This should not be thrown together in a single session but rehearsed properly over a longer period of time. Elements such as costume, make-up, lighting, sound and scenery will enhance your performance, but beware of spending too much time on the effects and neglecting the performance. Set a performance date when each group performs its piece for the others as though it is a public performance, not just a classroom exercise.

This exercise, if you spend sufficient time and effort in completing it and do not show or discuss your rehearsal process with the other groups, will give you a taste of what it is like to perform in front of an outside audience. Although you can analyse your work during rehearsals and change and improve things, you can only find out whether it works in performance when it has been before an audience. Even then, different things work for different audiences and the same production may get entirely different reactions at different performances.

Examining the performances

Before you discuss the performances with other groups, get together with your own group.

Examining your own performance

Discuss, with your group, how you think your performance went. The following are some suggestions for discussion points, but feel free to discuss any other points that come up in your discussion:

1. Did your performance go according to plan? If not, what was different?
2. Did you feel as though you communicated your performance effectively to your audience?
3. Did your audience react as you expected them to? If there were reactions you did not expect or no reactions where you expected them, why do you think this was?
4. Do you believe you all maintained concentration and kept in character for the whole performance?
5. Which areas do you believe went particularly well and which do you think should be improved? How would you improve these areas?

Once you have examined your own performance, discuss the performances of other groups.

Examining the performances of others

In the same way, discuss how effective you believe the performances of the other group or groups were from your point of view as an audience member. Remember that criticism is only useful if it is constructive and helpful – just saying that something is 'bad' or 'good' is of little use unless you can say why. The following are some suggested areas of discussion:

1. Could you see and hear everything that was important in the performance? Was the performance communicated effectively to the audience or were there areas that were unclear?
2. Did the performers maintain concentration and keep acting the characters, even when the focus of the scene was not on them?
3. Was the pace of the performance good or were there times when it appeared to drag or be rushed?
4. Were the actors and scenery arranged to create an effective stage picture appropriate to the scene or

were there times when it appeared untidy, unclear or not directed to the audience?

5. Was the story put over in a way that made it easy to follow and understand?

6. Which areas do you think were particularly effective and which did not work so well? How would you improve these areas?

Following these discussions, you should all get together again and report your findings to each other. Now you can tell others what you thought of their work and find out what others thought of yours. Try to listen to others' opinions of what you have done without leaping to defend it – if you have to justify or explain what you have done then maybe your performance was not as clear as it should have been. Some performers believe that if an audience does not 'get' their work then it must be due to a lack of intelligence on the audience's part, rather than any deficiencies in the performance. This is not a useful attitude to take if you want to learn or improve from your experiences. Of course, having listened to the opinions of others, you can still choose to disagree with them and do what you want, but at least you are doing so armed with the knowledge of how some people will see it.

Your own performances

Continuous assessment

In the above exercise, you assessed your final performance at the end. However, you would have been constantly assessing your ideas and performances while you were rehearsing your piece in order to try to improve it. Any performer or director should be constantly going through his or her performance and ideas, both inside and outside the rehearsal room, to see where improvements can be made. A useful way of formalising this process, which is required for some courses and examinations, is to keep a personal production diary. After each rehearsal, write down what you have achieved and record your personal thoughts about how the rehearsals are going, where problems are arising and where you think you need to improve. Keep a note of where ideas come from, why you used or didn't use them and where you have used research. Writing this information down rather than carrying it around in your head forces you to organise your thoughts and specify exactly what you should be working on and where you see the rehearsals going. It can also provide a useful point of reference during rehearsals to see what you need to do next and can be invaluable if you have to write an essay or sit an examination based on this project.

Final assessment

This is where you examine the whole of your project in detail and assess how it went. This may have to be submitted in the form of an essay or it may be used to formulate your thoughts and remind you of details for a written examination or oral assessment. There are certain key points that you should cover:

1. **What you did** – A detailed description of your piece and how and why you chose it.
2. **How you did it** – The process that you went through, how you got the ideas, details of your research, why you selected some ideas and discarded others, how you arranged the ideas and how you created the characters.
3. **How it went** – How the audience reacted, whether it went as you hoped or expected, what was particularly effective, what didn't work so well and how you would improve it if you did it again.

Write in as much detail as you can, referring to specific moments in your piece and avoiding generalisations such as, 'it could have been better if we had tried harder' or 'we needed to work on the first scene more'. You need to say what you would have done to that first scene to improve it, where you weren't trying hard enough and what would you try to do better next time.

Watching a play

Going to the theatre

Earlier in this chapter, you looked at another group's performance and assessed it. When you go to the theatre to watch a play, there are many more things that you can take into account in your assessment. Some people worry that analysing a play will take away the enjoyment of watching it, but being able to see how a performance works can give you greater enjoyment and a much deeper understanding of the play, as well as a greater appreciation of the work of the people who created it. An ability to analyse drama may make you less tolerant of poorly constructed and performed drama in the theatre, on television and at the cinema. Once you are able to determine how certain effects are achieved on stage, you will be able to add them to your toolbox of things you can use in your own productions.

Just as in documenting your own productions, you should make as many notes as you can at every stage of your experience. The following are some important areas for you to note, roughly in the order you will come across them.

The play

The vast majority of modern drama, on stage and screen, begins with a script. For you to effectively assess how the production has turned the script into a performance, you should get hold of a copy of the script and study it carefully. If the play is not script based, find out where its ideas and storylines came from. A lot of devised theatre is based on existing factual or fictional stories. The programme is sometimes a good source of information about the play and production. Break the play down into small sections as described in chapter 3 and briefly summarise the action in each of these sections. Next to this, give a detailed description of what you saw *in the production* during each section – in other words everything that you saw and heard when you watched the play that wasn't stated specifically in the script. This should include notes on acting, movement, set, lighting, make-up, music, sound effects and anything else relevant to that moment in the production as in Fig. 27.

In this way, you can separate the play as written by the playwright from the production so that you can work out what choices were made by the director, actors and others on

▶
Fig. 27:
Example
breakdown of
first episode of
Our Country's
Good by
Timberlake
Wertenbaker,
directed by Max
Stafford-Clark

Episode	Script	Production
Act I Scene 1: The Voyage Out	Sideway is being flogged as Clark counts the lashes. Wisehammer and Arscott describe the appalling conditions on the convict ship.	The convicts are all huddled together in semi-darkness on a platform hanging from the ceiling, which is swaying gently to give the impression of them being on a ship. Sideway is seen being flogged in silhouette behind a white half curtain upstage. The actors speak their lines with little expression, directly to the audience.

the production team and decide how effective and relevant those choices were.

Many people prefer to do this preparatory work before seeing a play as they are armed with a knowledge and understanding of the play and can see easily what has been added by the production team. However, you should be aware that your reactions to a production will be very different if you see it with little or no knowledge of the script. If you save your script analysis until after you have seen the play, you will probably miss some things as everything is new to you. An ideal situation would be to see the play at least twice and to do your script analysis in between, which also allows you to examine how the production differs at different performances before different audiences. This is not always practically or financially possible.

The theatre

When writing about a production, the theatre building is often forgotten. However, the location and design of the theatre building contributes a great deal to the experience the audience has, as well as influencing what types of plays are produced there and what types of audiences it attracts. If the play is touring, it may have to be adapted to fit the space, and the same production may look and feel very different if you see it at a different venue.

Where is the theatre – in a city centre, in the countryside, in a student area, in the suburbs, in a room over a pub, in the middle of a housing estate? Is it amateur or professional? Is it a producing theatre (one that has its own resident theatre company) or a receiving house (one that is visited by touring companies) or a combination of the two? Is it a proscenium theatre, a studio theatre, a black box theatre or a very modern design? Does the design appear to be trying to attract people of a certain age group or social class? What type of acting space does the theatre have (see page 11).

Audience

A look at the audience may give an indication of how the production has been publicised or what sort of person is attracted by this theatre or type of play. Different audiences will react differently to the same production, which may influence how the actors perform (theatre is two-way communication).

Is it a full house or are there a lot of empty seats (also note which day of the week it is and whether it is an evening, matinee or morning performance)? Are there a lot of people from a particular age group, ethnic group or gender? Are most people dressed formally or casually? Is the audience quiet and attentive or is there a lot of talking, rustling of sweet wrappers and movement? How does the audience react to the performance? Are there times when you believe their reactions to be inappropriate or where you believe they should have reacted but didn't? Listening in to people's conversations at the interval and when you are leaving can sometimes be quite revealing.

Performances

Distinct from the choices made by the production is how well the performers actually put over these choices to the audience. Were the actors appropriate for the roles they were playing? Did they communicate their characters and the scenes effectively to the audience? Were there any obvious problems or mistakes in the performance and, if so, how were they dealt with?

Design and technical

You should have made some notes about how the design worked in specific moments of the play but there are some general points to consider. Was there a specific style to the design of the production (including set, lighting, costume, make-up and sound)? Did the design add to the play's message and story or distract from it? Did the style of the design fit with the style of the acting? Did it bring out themes of the play that would not otherwise have been so obvious? Was it different from how you expected it to be?

Writing your review

These notes show what you actually experienced when you went to see the production. When you come to write your review of the play, you need to make connections between different aspects of the production and formulate your opinions. Look at specific moments in the play and work out why you believe the actors did certain things and whether you think their actions were effective. Always back up your opinions with specific references to parts of the script and production. If you believe something did not work, state why and how you think it could have been done better. Do not forget that all of the aspects of a production mentioned above contribute in some way to its effectiveness and can be used to justify your opinions and arguments.

Writing an essay

Answering the question

This may seem so obvious that it is not worth mentioning, but it is actually a trap that a great many people fall into. It is very easy to get so wrapped up in your arguments and ideas that you wander off at tangents and write about things that are nothing to do with the question you have been asked. If you do this for an essay or examination, you will waste time writing information for which you will get no marks.

One way of avoiding this is to write an essay plan before you start. In an examination this may appear to use up valuable time, but your plan can be a very brief outline to give you a logical structure to follow. Each chapter of this book began as a series of headings jotted down with a few notes about what could be included. Your essay plan is not carved in stone and can be changed if you think of something better when you are writing, but whenever you stop to wonder where to go next your plan can help you. It should also help to give your essay a structure and form that would be more difficult to achieve if you just wrote off the top of your head.

Essay structure

The following is a very simple structure that can be used or adapted for most essay-type questions.

Introduction

State *what* you intend to discuss or argue in your essay and *why* you are doing this (in other words why you believe your argument to be important, not 'because the question has asked me to').

Main body of essay

This is where you describe your points in detail and argue them, backing up your arguments with references to the text or the performance. Give each point its own paragraph and construct each paragraph as follows:

- State your point or observation
- Develop your argument using specific examples and references from the script or production
- End by showing the relevance of your point to your overall argument and the essay question.

Conclusion

Bring together the points made at the end of each paragraph and use them to answer the question. A really good essay will also look at the implications of your findings beyond the material you have studied.

Tutorial

Practice questions

1 For a piece of drama that you were involved in as a performer or designer and that was performed before an audience, describe how your group worked together to create the piece and assess how effective it was in performance. How would you improve it if you could work on it further?

2 For a theatre production you have seen, describe two acting performances and give reasons why you believe these performances were effective or ineffective. Give specific examples from the production to show your reasons.

Student assignment

Collect theatre reviews from newspapers and magazines and look at how the different reviewers approach reviewing a play. Look in particular at reviews of plays – or even films and television programmes – that you have seen and compare the reviewer's opinions with your own.

Further Reading

If you wish to study any of the areas covered by this book in more depth, the following books and websites will be useful to you.

Books

What is theatre?

Wickham, Glynne; *A History of the Theatre* (Oxford: Phaidon, 1985)
A standard reference work on theatre history.

Hartnoll, Phyllis (ed); *The Oxford Companion to the Theatre* (Oxford: Oxford University Press, 1967)

Hartnoll, Phyllis; *The Theatre: A Concise History* (London: Thames & Hudson, 1985)

Brown, John Russell (ed); *The Oxford Illustrated History of Theatre* (Oxford: Oxford University Press, 1995)
General reference works on theatre.

Eyre, Richard & Nicholas Wright; *Changing Stages: A view of British theatre in the twentieth century*
A very selective look at theatre history, written to accompany the BBC TV series of the same name.

Improvisation

Johnstone, Keith; *Impro: Improvisation and the theatre* (London: Methuen, 1979)
An inspirational and entertaining book on creating theatre that should be read and re-read by anyone teaching or learning about theatre.

Goldberg, Andy; *Improv Comedy* (Hollywood: Samuel French, 1991).
Plenty of information about how to practise and perform improvised comedy plus a good selection of exercises.

Working with scripts

Benedetti, Jean; *Stanislavski and the Actor* (London: Methuen, 1998)
Benedetti has filtered the writings of Stanislavski and others that knew and worked with him into this practical book, which describes many of Stanislavski's techniques including the use of the Method of Physical Actions in rehearsal.

Brecht, Bertolt; *Collected Plays: Five;* Edited and introduced by John Willett and Ralph Manheim (London: Methuen, 1995)
This book contains two of Brecht's major plays, and in the back is a translation of Brecht's notes on his own production of Mother Courage and her Children, *which is extremely useful for showing how Brecht turned a script into a performance.*

Designing the stage

Thomas, Terry; *Create Your Own Stage Sets* (London: A & C Black, 1985)
A very practical guide to designing and building sets.

Goodison, John (ed); *British Theatre Design: The Modern Age* (London: Phoenix Illustrated, 1993)
This book is filled with photographs and drawings of scenery, costumes and model boxes for different types of productions.

Lighting

Reid, Francis; *The Stage Lighting Handbook* (London: A & C Black, 1996)
Considered by many to be the standard book for learning about stage lighting. Regularly updated and well explained.

Sound

Leonard, John A.; *Theatre Sound* (London: A & C Black, 2001)
An excellent book covering all aspects of sound that any theatre sound designer or technician should know in detail.

White, Paul; *Live Sound for the Performing Musician* (London: Sanctuary, 1998)

Although aimed at musicians and therefore not containing anything specifically about designing sound for the theatre, this book explains the principals of live sound and the equipment used in a very clear and easy-to-understand way.

Writing about theatre

Theatre Record (London)
This journal reprints, in full, reviews by the major national drama critics of all theatre productions in London and many regional productions. Larger libraries may have both current and old copies of the journal, which can be very useful for researching different productions of the same play.

Warning

We are pointing you towards these websites as a matter of courtesy, but neither Studymates Limited nor the author nor any/all of their agents can be held responsible for the outcome(s) of any interaction, whether in person, or via any other means including electronic interaction, with these sites. **Readers are advised to take professional advice, where appropriate, before entering into any commitments with those listed here.**

Website reviews compiled by the author

British Theatre Guide
www.britishtheatreguide.info
News, reviews and articles relating to theatre in the UK.

What's On Stage
www.whatsonstage.com
An extensive database of current productions around the UK together with news, reviews and a facility to buy tickets online.

Didaskalia: Ancient Theater Today
didaskalia.open.ac.uk
A huge amount of information on ancient Greek and Roman theatre.

Shakespeare's Globe
www.shakespeares-globe.org
The official website of Shakespeare's Globe, a modern reconstruction in London of a theatre where many of Shakespeare's plays were first performed.

Improv Encyclopedia
www.humanpingpongball.com
Lots of information about improvisation together with many games and exercises.

International Brecht Society
german.lss.wisc.edu/brecht
The website of a society dedicated to researching the work of Brecht.

Project 2000 National Theatre Design Archive
www.siue.edu/ITDA
A project to put the work of theatre designers on the World Wide Web for others to see.

PLASA (Professional Lighting and Sound Association)
www.plasa.org
Official website of the UK-based organisation and its magazine, Lighting and Sound International.

The Theatre-Sound Mailing List Home Page
www.brooklyn.com/theatre-sound
An email list for those involved with sound in the theatre.

Theatre Sound Manufacturers Links
www.auldworks.com/theater/proaud1.htm
A huge list of links to websites of audio equipment manufacturers.

The MiniDisc Community Portal
www.minidisc.org
A site devoted entirely to news and information about Minidiscs.

Sounddogs.com
www.sounddogs.com
A website with a huge collection of sound effects that can be previewed at low quality and then purchased online and downloaded at professional quality.

Controlbooth.com
www.controlbooth.com/index.html
An American site for teaching technical theatre subjects to high school and college students.

Extra website reviews compiled for Studymates by James Craig B.A.

Drama

Don't just think of drama courses in terms of acting. A good course will also develop your confidence, develop your ability to 'perform' on stage and open a huge amount of opportunities. It is worth remembering that most people are terrified of public speaking. That means you are already at an advantage. According to the businessman Ted Nicholls, 51% of Americans state public speaking is their biggest fear. That means more people would prefer to be in the casket at a funeral than to give the eulogy!

So think 'outside the box'. TV presenters are often actors, conference presenters similarly are also often actors and many radio broadcasters started out as actors, so there are huge opportunities for you.

Oxford Advanced Studies program

www.oasp.ac.uk/pgya/subjects/2004/drama.htm

This looks very interesting. Have a look and decide for yourself.

Aberyswyth University

www.aber.ac.uk/~drawww/ucaspracexp.html

There isn't a great deal on this website but if you fancy 3 great years at university in what is one of the most beautiful places in the United Kingdom, (Make no mistake you will fall in love with that part of West Wales), then this is worth considering. The university is well respected but this is all they have to say on their site:

When selecting applicants the Department will look for evidence of a practical interest in the relevant area of study.

Although the aquisition of practical drama skills is not at present a formal pre-requisite of entry onto the degree prospective you are encouraged to gain some experience of the practical areas of performance or drama (e.g. amateur dramatics, professional performance, dance, movement, design or technical work).

Central School of Speech and Drama
www.cssd.ac.uk/courses/undergraduate/drama_applied_theatre_education.htm

This is well worth your time. They are THE place in the U.K. to study drama.

Here is what they say:

This internationally renowned course is intended for students interested in studying the practice and theory of drama and theatre within a range of social, community and educational contexts. It is the key course in the country for such work and our graduates lead the field in community drama nationally. The employment rate among them is exceptionally high. The course also serves as a rigorous grounding for postgraduate studies in theoretical and practical drama, whether here at Central or elsewhere. Recent graduates have pursued postgraduate courses in drama therapy, classical acting, drama and theatre studies, teaching drama and theatre for development, amongst others.

Anglia Polytechnic University
web.apu.ac.uk/english/Drama%20APU%20in%20Cambridge.htm

Here is what they say:

All Single and Combined Honours Courses at APU are designed as 'modules' – hence we offer a 'modular' degree. Each module that you complete successfully will gain you either 10, 20 or, for some major practical Drama modules, 30 credits. Full-time students accumulate 120 credits per year; over three years this adds up to 360 credits, the amount that you need for your Honours degree.

APU is a highly respected institution and is well regarded by employers because of the quality of their graduates. If you do consider APU you will also have the pleasure of living in the delightful city of Cambridge. We think this is worthy of your consideration.

Royal Welsh College of Music and Drama

http://www.rwcmd.ac.uk/courses/ba_acting.asp

BA (Hons) Acting
Three Years, Full Time
Validated by the University of Wales
Accredited by the National Council for Drama Training

This looks like an excellent option for someone wanting to consider a degree in acting. This is what they have to say:

Public Performance

We stage 15 productions each year, ranging from intimate contemporary pieces to large-scale Shakespeare and Broadway musicals. Our performances take place in the college's own theatre spaces and the major professional theatres around Wales. Touring productions play at venues in London, Belfast and Dublin. We also commission new writing in both English and Welsh, giving you the opportunity to perform in cutting-edge drama.

Sheffield University

http://www.shef.ac.uk/literature/ugmodules/lit184.html

They say:

Practical Drama offers you the opportunity to participate in a staff-directed production of a pre 20th century play text. The module is structured to allow you to explore, through practical workshops and related research, the complex process through which a text is rehearsed and performed. Students will also gain hands-on experience of basic health and safety skills appropriate to practical and studio-based work.

Whilst their website is minimalist, it is a well-respected university.

Chalkface Project

http://www.chalkface.com/category_Drama.html

Lesson plans and resources for drama teachers

Royal Shakespeare Company

http://www.rsc.org.uk/home/339.aspx

Well worth a look for any budding thespian. If Shakespeare is your thing (and lets face it, how many of us would not want to be in a Shakespeare drama?) make sure you get a copy of *Shakespeare: the barriers removed* by Dr Paul Innes, also published by Studymates1-84285051-2.

Redbridge Drama Centre

www.redbridgedramacentre.co.uk/

Redbridge children's youth and adult theatre workshops

Churchfields
South Woodford
London
E18 2RD
Email: rdc@redbridgedramacentre.co.uk
Telephone: 020 8504 5451
Fax: 020 8505 6669

University of East Anglia

www.uea.ac.uk/menu/study_and_research/undergrad/ugprospectus/subjects/drama.html#W400

BA Drama

This looks excellent and is worthy of your consideration if you want to study drama at university level. Here is what they say:

> *This programme allows you to combine a strong practical emphasis with the study of the theory, history and social significance of drama. This work is complemented by detailed study of dramatic literature and aspects of visual and technical design. You will participate in a major practical project each*

year as well as undertaking a wide variety of applied drama work; and there is also the opportunity for you to study on placement with professional companies. Our Studio Theatre hosts visiting professional companies as well as serving as the main teaching centre. We employ an interview and audition process for applicants to this programme. Overseas applicants who are unable to attend an audition should be willing to submit a video performance of specified audition pieces.

The Cuny School of Professional Studies at University Center

CUNY is the City University of New York
sps.gc.cuny.edu/kaplan/programs.html
Creating Theatre with Young People

This is most impressive and worthy of your consideration, especially if you live in North America.

Here is what they say:

Successful development and production of original theatre with young people requires a thorough understanding of student-centered pedagogy and the devising process, actor-centered directing skills, and comfort working with young people. Moreover, educators and artists engaged in this work must be able to apply all of this in practice.

University of Melbourne
www.unimelb.edu.au/HB/subjects/483-125.html

This is good and is most certainly of interest if you are in Australia. The website itself is a little formal but don't let that put you off because the University has an excellent international reputation.

Australearn Canada
www.australearncanada.org

This is the Canadian Center for Australian, New Zealand and South Pacific Universities.

Australearn USA

www.australearn.org

This is the North American Center for Australian, New Zealand and South Pacific Universities.

Drama New Zealand

www.drama.org.nz

This is an association of teachers, youth theatre and theatre in education practitioners who are interested in promoting the recognition, study and development of drama in education from early childhood to tertiary education. For any NZ based readers this is a must.

Queensland Tertiary Admissions Centre

www.qtac.edu.au/Publications/Information_Sheets/NCEA.htm

They say:

> QTAC is a non profit, public company established in 1990 by the six State universities that existed in Queensland at that time. QTAC now services 16 institutions.

On the day we visited their site they were actively seeking students from New Zealand and surrounding areas.

Christchurch College of Education

www.cce.ac.nz/

Not the most attractive of websites but they do have some very interesting courses in drama.

Toi Whakaari/ New Zealand Drama School

www.tewhaea.org.nz/toiwhakaari/toiwhakaari-home.html

This is what they say on their website:

> Toi Whakaari's philosophy is to provide exceptionally talented students with the skills to apply their imagination and intelligence to the realities of a career in the performing arts.
> This excellence is maintained by having some of New Zealand's most respected actors, technical specialists and

directors as tutors, and through having a rigorous enrolment policy.

They say they are New Zealand's foremost trainer in dramatic arts; if you are NZ based, this is certainly worth a consideration.

New Zealand Theatre

www.zeroland.co.nz/new_zealand_theater.html

It does exactly what it says; make sure it is listed in your favourites.

Auckland University NZ

www.arts.auckland.ac.nz/subjects/index.cfm?S=S_DRAMA

This is a very formal/institutional site but it does give you some idea of the courses available and the university itself does have an excellent international reputation.

Artscalendar.co.nz

http://www.artscalendar.co.nz/category/2/

An essential in your favourites, the sheer amount of information about New Zealand's arts in this website makes it impressive.

Helen O Grady Childrens Drama Academy

www.helenogrady.com

This is an international organisation that provides drama for 5 to 17 year olds. They have offices around the world and help young people develop confidence and self-esteem, through drama. They appear to be particularly strong in the Southern hemisphere. As educators ourselves, we were impressed with what they have to offer.

The New School for Drama

www.newschool.edu/academic/drama

They are located at
151 Bank Street
New York, NY 10014
212.229.5859

US based readers should have a good look at this site, what they are offering looks good.

The Juilliard School

www.juilliard.edu

They are located at
60 Lincoln Center Plaza
New York, NY 10023-6588
(212) 799-5000

We were extremely impressed by their public school education program. This organisation reaches out and engages young people in the arts and that is truly to be applauded.

The Drama League

www.dramaleague.org

Here is what they say on their site

> Since 1916, The Drama League has been a second home for those who love American theatre. Founded as an association of theatre professionals and patrons dedicated to encouraging the finest in professional theatre, The Drama League soon found news roles – as a service organization for theatre lovers interested in enhancing their understanding and experience of live theatre, and as an unparalleled training program for emerging theatre artists.

Check it out; it certainly looks good to us.

BELARIE HYMAN ZATZMAN B.A., M.A., Ph.D.

www.yorku.ca/bzatzman/dramalinks.htm

A number of excellent links here, they are mainly Canadian and worth a look.

Victoria University Canada

www.educ.uvic.ca/edci/I9-drama.htm

Lots of links regarding drama and we like links, they are very helpful.

This is also a well-respected university so if you are based in Canada and thinking about University, then this has to be on your list.

The very nature of the internet means it is constantly changing. Therefore by necessity this can only be a selection of what is available. If you have any other sites you recommend do email the publishers at drama sites@studymates.co.uk and we will put them on the site and in the new edition of this book.

Liverpool
Community
College

Glossary of Terms

accepting Taking what another person says or does in an improvised scene and developing from it. See also *blocking*.

act *(verb)* To perform a role in the theatre. *(noun)* A large subdivision of a play. See also *scene*.

actor A person who performs in a scene or play. Can be male or female.

actress A female *actor*.

advance bar Lighting *bar* hung over the *auditorium*.

amplifier A device for turning low-level signals from various types of electrical sound equipment into speaker level signals to drive *loudspeaker* systems.

apron An area of stage in front of the *proscenium arch*.

aside A line in a play spoken directly to the audience that the other characters on stage do not hear.

audience People who have come to watch a performance.

auditorium The area that the audience occupies in a theatre. Literally 'hearing place'.

bar Horizontal metal tubing for hanging lighting instruments and other equipment from.

barn doors Hinged flaps attached to the front of certain types of *lantern* to limit the spread of the beam.

batten	(1) Long trays of *floods*, often used for lighting backcloths. (2) Lengths of timber at the top and bottom of cloths to stretch them out or used to fix *flats* together.
blackout	Turn off all stage *lanterns*.
blocking	(1) Not *accepting* what another person says or does in an improvised scene. Usually brings the *improvisation* to a halt. (2) The arrangement of *actors* on a stage. (3) Obscuring the audience's view of an *actor*.
boom	Vertical metal tubing for hanging lighting instruments from.
border	Horizontal strips of fabric used to frame the top of the stage and to hide technical equipment from the audience's view.
chase	A sequence of programmed lighting *states* stepped through automatically and usually repeated using a programmable lighting console.
chorus	In Greek theatre, a group of people that told the story to the audience. Now often used to describe any crowds of people on stage, particularly if they sing together.
circle	The balcony seats in a theatre *auditorium*.
compact disc (CD)	A digital recording medium read by a laser.
corpse	To laugh (as an actor) inappropriately during a performance.

crossfade	A transition from one lighting state to another.
cyc, cyclorama	A stretched cloth used as the backdrop to the stage, which can be coloured using lighting or have images projected onto it.
dark	A theatre is 'dark' when it is currently closed to the public. Many theatres go dark during the summer months.
devised production	A production created using improvisation during rehearsals rather than from a script.
dimmer	The device that controls the amount of power supplied to a stage *lantern*, thereby controlling its brightness.
downstage	The part of the stage nearest to the audience. See also *upstage, stage left, stage right*.
dry	(As an actor) To forget one's lines.
end stage	A stage at one end of a room with all the audience facing it from the same side.
equalisation (EQ)	The tone of a sound, split into different frequency bands for adjustment.
fader	A control on a sound or lighting desk to vary the level of sound or light.
flat	A timber frame covered with canvas or plywood, painted and used as scenery.
floats	Another name for *footlights*, from their origin as candles floating in a trough of water.

flood

Simple stage *lanterns* that flood an area with light.

follow spot

A *lantern* controlled by an operator to follow performers on the stage.

footlights

Lighting at the front of the stage shining up at the actors. Used to be very common but not often used in modern lighting design.

found space

A space used for performance that was built for a purpose other than theatre, such as a factory or warehouse, which uses the existing architecture of the building rather than converting it into a theatre.

fourth wall

A concept in naturalistic theatre in which the *proscenium arch* opening is treated as one of four walls in a room and the presence of the audience is not acknowledged by the actors.

Fresnel

A stepped lens used in a stage *lantern* of the same name giving a soft, unfocused beam.

front of house (FOH)

The areas of the theatre where the audience is.

gauze

A type of stage cloth that appears opaque when lit from the front but which becomes semi-transparent when lit behind.

gel

Coloured plastic placed in front of the beam of a *lantern* in order to colour it.

gobo

A cut metal or printed glass disc inserted into a *profile* in order to project an image or break up the light beam.

gods	Nickname for the seats on the highest balcony in an *auditorium* that usually cost the least.
groundrow	Low scenery placed on the stage. Also rows of lighting placed on the stage floor, often concealed by scenic groundrows.
heavens	The canopy over the stage in a public theatre in Renaissance London.
hell	The area under the stage in a public theatre in Renaissance London from which sounds of ghosts and devils often emanated.
improvisation	Creating drama without a script, at least partly making it up during the performance.
intelligent lighting	Lighting fixtures with functions that can be remotely controlled such as colour, *pan* and *tilt* (for moving lights), *gobo*, focus and *iris*.
iris	A device inserted into a *profile* to enable the size of the beam to be varied.
ladder	Vertical structure that looks like a ladder for hanging lighting instruments.
lamp	The light source (bulb) in a stage *lantern*.
lantern	A stage lighting instrument.
leg	Vertical strips of fabric used to mask the audience's view into the wings.

light curtain	A solid wall of light produced by a bank of *parcans* in a line facing straight down.
loudspeaker (speaker)	A device for turning electrical signals into sound waves.
microphone (mic)	A device for turning sound waves into electrical signals.
MIDI	Musical Instrument Digital Interface. A method for electronic instruments and other equipment such as keyboards, sound modules, sequencers, effects units and computers to communicate with one another.
mute	Block all sound output from a particular channel.
noise boy	Slang for sound engineer.
on the book	In charge of the master script marked with everybody's cues.
open white (O/W)	A *lantern* with no *gel* to colour its beam.
opposite prompt (OP)	*Stage right*, the side opposite where the *prompt* traditionally sits.
orchestra	The central floor area of a Greek theatre in which most of the play was staged. Also used in the USA to refer to the ground floor of the *auditorium*, known as the *stalls* in the UK.
pan	Short for 'panorama'. Locating a sound in the stereo sound field by varying how much of the sound goes to each of the right and left speaker outputs. The control for adjusting pan on a sound mixer is often referred to as a 'pan pot' ('pot' is short for

'potentiometer', which is a kind of variable resistor). Also the name of the function on moving lights to rotate the beam between left and right (see also *tilt*).

parcan	A simple *lantern* producing an oval, parallel beam from a *lamp* with a built-in parabolic reflector.
perches	Lighting instruments fixed to or immediately behind the *proscenium arch*.
prepared improvisation	A piece of drama created using improvisation and rehearsed.
producing theatre	A theatre building with its own theatre company to create productions. See also *receiving house*.
profile	A type of stage *lantern* containing a lens or series of lenses to sharply focus the beam.
promenade	A stage configuration in which each scene takes place in a different place and the audience moves to see it.
prompt	(1) The person *on the book* who feeds a line to an actor if they *dry* during a performance or rehearsal. (2) Also the name given to a line given to an actor by the person *on the book* to remind them where they are up to. (3) *Stage left*, the side of the stage the prompt traditionally sits. Sometimes denoted by 'P' in old scripts.
proscenium; proscenium arch	A type of end stage with an arch or picture frame around it. Also the name for the frame.

public address (PA) Equipment for amplifying sound through *loudspeakers* in a public environment.

pyrotechnics Stage fireworks, from bangs, coloured smoke and brightly-coloured flashes to confetti bombs.

rake A slope on the stage that rises away from the audience.

receiving house A theatre that receives touring productions but does not create its own productions. See also *producing theatre*.

scene A subdivision of a play or *act* forming a complete unit.

script The written text on which a performance is based.

sequencer A device for recording sequences of MIDI information and playing them back to control electronic musical instruments and other equipment.

shutters Metal blades in *profiles* that can be used to alter the size and shape of the beam.

skene The building on one side of the *orchestra* in a Greek theatre in which the actors changed; it was also used as scenery.

soliloquy A speech by a solo character to the audience, speaking his or her thoughts.

sound reinforcement The use of amplified sound in a live environment.

spontaneous improvisation	An improvised scene made up on the spot without any prior preparation.
stage left; stage right	The left or right of an *actor* stood in the centre of the stage facing the audience. See also *upstage, downstage*.
stalls	The lowest level of seating in an *auditorium*, known as the *orchestra* in America.
state	A fixed pattern of lights at various brightnesses.
status	A measure of how dominant or submissive each character is in a scene. This is not necessarily related to social status, and can change within a scene.
tab warmers	Lighting used to highlight the main *tabs* – the front curtains – for when the audience comes in and goes out.
tabs (tableau curtains)	Stage curtains – especially those that come in from both sides and overlap in the middle.
theatre-in-education (TIE)	Theatre work with specific educational aims, used as an educational resource by schools and colleges. See also *young people's theatre*.
theatre-in-the-round	A stage configuration in which the audience completely surrounds a circular acting space.
theatron	The seating in a Greek theatre which surrounded the *orchestra*.
thespian	Another name for an *actor*, from Thespis of Ancient Greece who was said to be the first actor.

thrust	A stage configuration in which the audience occupies three of the four sides of either the whole acting space or an area that extends forward from it.
tilt	The function on moving lights for rotating the beam up and down.
tiring house	The building behind the stage from which the *actors* made their entrances in a public theatre in Renaissance London.
traverse	A stage configuration in which the audience occupies two opposing sides of the acting space.
truck	A wheeled platform that can be set with scenery and / or *actors* to help with quick changes of set.
upstage	The part of the stage furthest away from the audience. See also *downstage*, *stage left*, *stage right*.
wigglies	Slang for moving *intelligent lights*.
wings	The areas on either side of the stage that are normally concealed from the audience's view.
wipe	A single curtain that comes across the stage on a single rail (as opposed to double *tab* curtains that meet in the middle).
young people's theatre (YPT)	A blanket term for theatre for or involving children and young people. See also *theatre-in-education*.

Index

Free Report Bonus #1

Creating New Drama

by James Craig BA

As a thank-you for buying and reading *Practical Drama*, Studymates commissioned James Craig (a writer of several books) to give you a bonus. We wanted to give you some extra information that will stimulate your thinking about drama and maybe even persuade you to have a go at writing drama when your course is over.

Here is James' report:

Practical Drama is a delight and that is why the people at Studymates were so keen to publish David Chadderton's book, but there is one more aspect that you need to consider and that is writing drama.

Good drama is well written and then well acted and this is why you might consider *Writing TV Scripts* by Steve Wetton, (isbn 1-84285-071-7). Steve wrote a major BBC series called *Growing Pains* back in the 1980's and was the driving force behind a number of other projects at BBC radio and television. He then went on to teach creative writing at Derby University for a number of years and is now back writing for top major UK talent. Steve Wetton has written for *The Lenny Henry Show*, *The Brian Conley Show* and *The Two Ronnies*, so he does know what he is talking about.

But is there a demand for new writing?

Think about the opportunities that are available for writers. There are hundreds of tv channels and they are all hungry for material for new programmes, there are hundreds of main theatres and smaller regional theatres that are hungry for new drama. The major BBC Radio speech based stations in the UK are always on the lookout for new drama. The same is true worldwide. In fact there has never been a better time to consider starting to write your own drama.

But Steve is quite pragmatic when dealing with new writers. He quite openly tells new writers that a script that is developed will not be recorded with actors and broadcast. In fact in his book he explains how this script will be your 'calling card'. By this he means it will be a vehicle to show your talent to producers, it is your way of selling yourself as a writer.

But can anyone write?

Well yes and no. That is not 'sitting on the fence' it is true. Not everyone can write but most people can certainly learn to write and you could be the same. It really could be your name on the credits of a top drama on tv or your play that is being performed in the West End of London or on Broadway and that is not a joke. Think about how that would make you feel, isn't it great!

For the rest of this report I am going to stick to tv because that is what I know most about and Steve Wetton's book is such a help. Think about tv, it is roughly a 50:50 split between speech and visuals. This will impact on your writing, even if you have written a page of speech the audience will still need something to see and the visuals will need to carry the story forward. Steve gives an example of a man nervously opening letters and then punching the air in triumph as he shouts out 'yes'. This immediately makes the character more interesting and most people will be intrigued by his behaviour. What does his behaviour suggest to you? Maybe he has just won a competition? Maybe he has got a job interview or actually got the job itself? But what if, as Steve suggests, he then covers his tracks by announcing to his wife (who is out of sight) that there was nothing unusual in the post. Immediately we start to see a new side to his character, he is hiding something but why? Is he having an affair? Is he involved in something illegal? Now think of what we have seen, a man opening his post. It is hardly the most exciting visual but the way it is written is incredibly dramatic.

Getting Started

Think of your own experiences. You must have heard it said that writers should 'write about what they know'. This makes a lot of sense it gives an authorial voice to your writing. If you live in an area you know how people talk, the nuances they give to their speech. You understand the local culture and this is something that you can write about. The author Lindsey Ashford is not an ex police officer so why does she write such good crime novels? Simply because she is a criminologist and so has expertise that she can draw on. You also have expertise, your experiences are unique to you and if you were to write them down they would be written in a way that others simply could not replicate, they would reflect your authorial voice.

One warning: if you are a young person do not try and write what it is like to be older. Older people can write what it is like to be young because they were young once BUT you have never yet been older so stick with what you know.

Look back in this book and ensure you understand how David Chadderton has used drama to convey emotion and feelings on stage or in a studio. Now adapt them for television. Think about the close up shot, how will the actor convey what he or she is feeling at that particular time?

The purpose of this report was to stimulate your thinking, to get you to consider another avenue for your talent in drama. It is often the case that the most successful performers are also writers and many go on to write full time for others.

Remember the law of the farm. First you have to sow then nurture before you can reap the rewards. Here we are encouraging you to consider writing as a possible extra to your repertoire of skills. If it is not for you then you have lost nothing BUT we hope that just maybe we have planted a germ of an idea for you to develop further.

James Craig
Studymates Limited

Free Bonus Report # 2
Improving Your Learning
By Graham Lawler MA

Again as a thank-you for buying and using this book we are giving you a free-value added bonus report.

As a person you need to keep learning, frankly regardless of how old you are at the moment. Learning improves us as people and the mark of a superior person is that she or he cares about and creates their own future by anticipating it and planning for it. But learning is hard work, so how can you learn to improve your own learning?

Avoidable mistake #1

I must work harder!

When people say this what they actually mean is they must put in more hours. Now this may be true; if you have been slacking, be honest with yourself and do something about it.

But the fact is that for many students and learners, they are simply overloaded with work. The reality of being a student means that many people have to work in part-time jobs, they are attending lectures/workshops/lessons and so the idea of spending more time studying is simply not possible.

So what is the answer?

The answer is to work smarter!

What is smarter working?

By working smarter we mean making the time you spend studying more effective. Just imagine that you could spend less time studying and get better grades, well you can.

How do I work smarter?

First of all you do need to invest some 'front-end loaded' time. You need to understand a little about how the brain works. British psychologist Tony Buzan invented a brilliant system to aid learning called mind mapping™. This is an information processing system that means you can literally achieve the effect of reading as many as 4 books in a day and remembering the key points. Studymates does not often recommend books by other publishers because the majority are simply not good enough but here we make an exception. We highly recommend

'*The Mind Map Book*' written by Tony Buzan and published by BBC books. Many town libraries have the book and many colleges and university libraries will also stock the book so it is worth your time to read and understand the system.

Avoidable mistake #2

' *I am rubbish at essays*'

First of all, stop and recognise that if this applies to you, then you are human, so re-frame the experience. It means you have completed part of a SWOT analysis. (We'll mention SWOT again later).

You have identified an area that you need to improve. In this book David Chadderton has given you excellent advice including writing but if you need more in-depth advice, look out for Dr Derek Soles book from Studymates, '*The Academic Essay*'(1-84285-065-2). Derek Soles is a recognised international expert on writing communication. He is a professor at a major US university and frankly if you need to improve your understanding of how to complete an essay, Derek's advice is invaluable. If you follow his advice and do what he says at each stage, then there is no doubt, your grades will go up.

What is a SWOT analysis?

SWOT is an acronym that stands for Strengths, weaknesses, opportunities, and threats. It is a standard tool that is often used in business and one that you can use to judge your own performance. What are your strengths?   What are your weaknesses (we all have them)? What opportunities exist for you?   What threats exist for you?

Avoidable mistake #3

' *I know it I just can't get it across*'

This is an explicit admission that your communication skills need to improve. This is a really easy one to solve. John Kennedy's book '*Study skills*' from Studymates (1-84285-064-4) explains all the skills needed to be a successful student, including how to give presentations. This is what we mean by 'front-end loading'. By investing the time to improve your skills you are ensuring your long-term success. Dr Stephen Covey tells the apocryphal story of a woodcutter who was sawing wood with a rusty saw. When it was pointed out to him that if he sharpened the saw he would be more effective, he replied ' I know but I can't, I haven't got the time'. Make certain that you 'sharpen your saw'. The skills you will learn from these books will vastly improve your performance as a student. It will also mean that you can spend less time studying and get better grades and that is a promise!

Graham Lawler
Studymates Limited